The Right Futu[re] for Florida and You... Starting Right Now!

"A Bold, New, Serious Vision for Progress and Prosperity to Position Florida in Our Rightful Leadership Role for Long-term Success"

Written by a single parent, soldier, educator, small-business owner, healthcare professional, farmer and proud American...

"Who Walks in Your Shoes"

Colonel Mike McCalister, Ph.D.

Table of Contents

Table of Contents

Author's Background

First, Mike is not a politician. He is a practicing professional in education and agriculture, and has over 30 years experience in military service and healthcare. He "walks the walk" just like you. He teaches university classes for working adults several nights each week. He works daily with the medical schools, teaching hospitals and doctors to bring products, better pricing, educational resources and patient aid materials to the medical community. Like many in agriculture, he is out in his palm tree farm on freezing nights trying to protect his crop, not just surveying someone's loss. **He is one of you, experiencing many of the same concerns and pains as you do.**

Mike came from a farming family with military roots. His grandfather served in WWI and his father and both uncles served in WWII, with one uncle receiving three Purple Hearts and the other killed in action at Guadalcanal. His father later was a small business owner selling farming equipment. Mike is a single parent with one son, William, who attended St. Pete College, USF College of Engineering and UF College of Law.

Personal Education

Mike earned a B.S. in science, with a major in agriculture at a small state university. He then completed the U.S. Army Command & General Staff College studying leadership, tactics and decision making. After completing a Ph.D. in Management from the Union Institute he graduated from the Air University War College, a senior DoD school, where he studied national security, policy and strategy, as well as the

1

Military-industrial complex. He then completed the Harvard University Program on Senior Executive Leadership at the JFK School of Government with focus on Managing for Maximum Performance, Decision Making During Times of Uncertainty, Creativity in Products and Services, and Communicating Effectively.

Military Duty

Mike served a total of 33 years in the military, first as an enlisted man, and then as a Combat Arms officer in the defense of our nation in the U.S. Army Reserves, National Guard and Active Duty. His assignments included Platoon Leader, Executive Officer, Commanding Officer, Communications Officer, Logistics Officer, Operations, Training, Personnel Officer, Environmental Officer and Active Duty positions including in the Center for Operations, Plans and Policy at the United States Special Operations Command involved in the War on Terror.

As an Active Duty Colonel, he chaired a global study for the Department of Defense on an issue of national security. Additionally Mike served as the Subject Matter Expert at a U.S. Congressional testimony on national security and military training, prepared "White Papers" on base closure issues and infrastructure investments, served on Pentagon committees and initiatives including representing U.S. Special Operations as a member of the Secretary of Defense Training Transformation Executive Steering Committee, and served as the Assessment Chief for U.S. Special Operations Forces overseas anti-terrorist training of foreign nation military forces.

Mike became known as a global expert on military readiness, training and education, and was often tasked to attend Pentagon strategic meetings involving infrastructure investment. In this assignment he was awarded the Legion of Merit, Defense Meritorious Service Medal, War on Terror Service Medal, National Defense Service Medal and Joint Meritorious Unit Medal.

Professional Education Experience

Mike has an extensive background serving schools, colleges and universities at all levels of education. He is currently an Advisory Board member for a charter elementary school (grades kindergarten through 8th grade), and is on the planning committee for a charter high school (grades 9 through 12). He taught military science, served on the Faculty Senate, was the Department Chair and on a Presidential Academic Task Force at Florida A & M University.

Mike has taught undergraduate and MBA courses at several Florida colleges and universities as an adjunct professor of business, including university MBA courses at multiple Florida hospitals (HCA, North Broward, and Baptist) for hospital executives, doctors, pharmacists, and nurses. He has chaired numerous MBA thesis committees and served on multiple doctoral dissertation committees at Florida universities. Additionally, Mike has served on curriculum development committees and has taught college business courses internationally. He has also instructed MBA courses that include Strategy & Policy, Implementing Organizational Objectives, Policy and Decision Making, Systems

Thinking, Operations Management, Human Resource Management, Marketing Management, Organizational Behavior, Project Management, International Business, Entrepreneurship, and Business Research Methods.

Healthcare Experience

Mike has worked in the healthcare arena for over two decades providing medical services, products and educational grants to doctors, hospitals, pharmacists, nurses and patients throughout Florida. This included positions as an institutional consultant, hospital representative and clinical science specialist. In these positions working for biotech and research pharmaceutical companies, Mike helped bring new life sustaining products to critically ill patients suffering from terminal diseases.

Much of his time was spent with specialty physicians, hospitals and pharmacies assisting with patient enrollments onto national registries, as well as third party payment and delivery of these newly researched critical biotech products. He worked to get better pricing and availability for medications to hospitals and patients, including helping patients enroll in compassionate use programs where they would receive life saving therapies free of charge. Working with providers and patients gives Mike a comprehensive first hand experience and perspective of Florida's need for high quality and affordable healthcare.

Author's Acknowledgements

Acknowledgements and appreciation are extended to the many scholars, practitioners, professionals, concerned citizens, and graduate program students who have spent countless hours researching, studying and analyzing a virtual plethora of studies, articles, interviews, published reports and data in many of the areas of interest addressed in this book.

Thanks go to the Masters and Doctoral students I had the honor to teach, whose research, analysis and contributions in topics critical to Florida and the nation included among others: Healthcare; Florida's Education System; Future Job Careers and the Economy; and the Global Economy and the Impact of Outsourcing. I also wish to express my gratitude to writer/editor Michelle Close Mills for her tireless work on this project.

Chapter 1
Where I Stand and My Vision
for Florida's Rightful Leadership Role

This chapter provides you, my fellow Floridians, a "quick read" summary of this book and my Bold, New and Serious Vision for Florida. More in-depth analyses of many topics and issues are addressed in the following chapters, which can easily be identified in the Table of Contents.

This book provides the overall strategic goals and objectives, as well as the functional strategies and tactics to achieve this critical "Plan for Progress and Prosperity."

Where I Stand as a Floridian and an American

I am a serious conservative who believes the founding fathers envisioned a government that supports and protects citizens without unnecessary intervention into their lives. I believe Americans have earned the right to hold their heads high anywhere on the globe. When any foreign nation is in real trouble, where do they look for help? The answer is: The United States of America. Ours is the one nation who as "The Land of the Free and the Home of the Brave" has the capabilities and will to project national power and provide help to any country in need. When I hear the Star Spangled Banner or the roar of our military fighters overhead, it makes my hair stand on end and brings a chill of national pride and confidence throughout my body.

To anyone who questions the role and image of the United States in the eyes of the world I like to refer to Tony Blair, the former British Prime Minister, who when asked by the media why he so supported the United States when there are those who question our problems at home, he so eloquently replied, "A simple way to take measure of a country is to look at how many want in and how many want out." It sure seems to this proud American that there are a lot more people wanting in here than wanting out!

As a retired Colonel, I believe in a strong National Defense and am pro Second Amendment. I support the Constitution for a fair and speedy trial; then upon due process, the prompt administration of court decisions for justice to be served, including capital punishment.

I believe we need less government that is more efficient, less wasteful, and operates on a balanced budget that will pave the way for lower taxes. I believe government must be pro-business and facilitate economic growth and prosperity in a free market, leading to the creation of good paying career jobs that will last. I am for tort reform, and believe there should be term limits on all public offices and on the total cumulative time an elected official can serve in public office, just like there is for military officers.

I believe in God, separation of church and state, and traditional family values. I am pro-life, and though I don't believe that government should interfere in the personal choices of its citizens, I believe that tax payers should not be responsible for paying for those choices.

I oppose off-shore drilling of Florida's coastlines within the three mile limit; and I oppose expanded drilling in the Gulf of Mexico inside the 200 mile exclusive economic zone, and as well as outside the zone. Since the technology is not fool proof, the environment can't afford to pay the price for its failure. Neither can we.

I believe we must do much better educating our children from kindergarten through college and graduate school, as well as upgrading technical training programs for professionals who prefer trade careers. We must meet the challenges of the future by assessing and seizing opportunities in the global economy. I believe our young professionals are our near term future, our school age children are our longer term future, and we must prepare all of them to be competitive for success.

I support democracy to the fullest, and believe the two party system must have meaningful primary elections so voters will have a serious say in choosing their political party candidates for general elections. I am a strong believer in State's rights and the stance of "Don't Tread on Me." I fully support the need for a free and democratic Cuba.

I am in favor of cleaning up the welfare system. We should stop rewarding able bodied individuals who manipulate the law to receive taxpayer resources that should be used for those who are truly in need. I believe in enforcing the Americans with Disabilities Act, to provide meaningful job training for disabled citizens so they may live dignified, productive lives, enabled to make the contributions they want to make.

I believe we must deal with the issue of immigration in a way that is just and fair, and anyone enjoying the benefits of living in this country needs to be here legally and contributing to the tax system.

In spite of global competition, I believe that Florida has the people, resources, and potential to become a much greater economic force. We must create opportunities and provide the support to put Floridians in a strong leadership role. We must get displaced workers back on the job now, enhance the value and role of women in the workplace, launch the careers of our young professionals into a competitive business world, and protect the environment for future generations.

Purpose of This Book... How to Get Where We Want to Be!

Friends and colleagues, this book has been written to provide you with current, real world information, perspectives and input on the most critical issues facing our families and the State of Florida as seen through the eyes, experience, and perspectives of a fellow Floridian whose adult life has been spent as a practicing professional. Pass this book around to your family, friends and colleagues. The objective is to get this word out to everyone you know. I would recommend reading the first few chapters completely to gain an overall feel of the book and then move on to the chapters that seem most interesting to you.

I am neither a politician nor a political party leader. I am not a lawyer, corporate executive, member of the elite, or privileged few. I do not owe any debts or favors to a political party or to corporations. What I am is a single parent, soldier, educator, small business owner, health care professional, farmer, and a proud American who is a concerned conservative citizen that is asking you to join me in this serious fight for our state's future. **I am one of you!** Since this state is made up of you, me and our families, it is a battle worth fighting, wouldn't you agree? The time is now, and we must do this the right way together. I don't like losing, and its time to get this thing back on the winning track right now!

Like you, I walk the walk everyday in the trenches of the critical fields and industries that are of great interest and concern to Floridians. I understand first hand what it's like to be in difficult situations, such as experiencing job elimination, single parenthood, or concern about my child's education and professional future in this highly competitive global economy.

This text will be fairly short and to the point to allow for quick and easy reading.

My Bold, New and Serious Vision for Florida

This Vision for Florida will be discussed in more detail in the following chapters. However, some of the key objectives of my Vision include the following:

1) Robust job growth with sustainability in business and industry to include: healthcare, education, energy, agri-business, manufacturing and technology.

2) Significantly enhanced job training for displaced workers, as well as those who prefer a trade or tech school in lieu of a college education.

3) A significantly improved education system that is strategically aligned and seamless from kindergarten through college and graduate school, providing curriculums and degrees that will be in demand for future high paying jobs.

4) Ensure military bases, VA facilities, clinics and hospitals remain open and functioning at full capacity.

5) Create career opportunities and a positive future for young professionals and their families.

6) A high quality of life for our senior citizens that meets their specific needs.

7) An integrated and aligned healthcare system that provides affordable, high quality and accessible healthcare to all Floridians.

8) A legal system that provides a business friendly environment for Florida's future economic growth, helps keep health care costs down, and encourages doctors and hospitals to remain fully operating in Florida.

9) More competition in the insurance industry that provides Floridians more choices for available, dependable and fairly priced insurance for their homes, cars and healthcare. Also, lower the risks of increased taxes to Floridians by getting state government back to being a regulatory agency, and less of an insurance provider.

10) Security of our homes, neighborhoods, and borders must continue to improve and immigration concerns addressed to reach a resolution that is just for everyone.

11) Develop and implement an effective master plan and strategy for Florida that integrates and brings to bear all instruments, capabilities, advantages and human resources in a strategically aligned and tactically sound effort for Florida.

12) Leadership in Florida state government that integrates and coordinates priorities and efforts of government at all levels (city, county, state); and strategically aligns these efforts to ensure interoperability that best meets the needs of Floridians.

13) Unity and alignment from all of Florida's twenty five U.S. Congressional representatives as well as both U.S. Senators. Our U.S. Congressional and Senate leaders must present a united front in Washington and fight for what is best for Florida's citizens, not a national political party agenda.

Where I Stand on Critical Issues Facing Florida

This section will identify several of the critical issues and challenges facing the citizens of Florida and provide a brief summary of solutions for these issues. They will also be discussed in greater detail in later chapters. A term that will be used in several chapters is "strategically aligned." Though it will be discussed in more detail later in the book, this term basically describes the process of ensuring that all goals, strategies, tactics, resources and efforts are coordinated throughout the system(s) or organization in order to maximize success and minimize waste.

Jobs and the Economy

These two issues are a top priority. We must develop Florida's workforce, industry and education into a strategically aligned machine that creates and places Floridians in sustainable high paying career jobs. These topics will be discussed in greater detail in Chapters 2, 3 and 5.

Issues: A totally unacceptable fragile state economy with an unemployment rate over 10% in many areas due to recession, outsourcing, off-shoring, government regulation, as well as the need for better job training and education. This environment has significantly contributed to the current devastating home foreclosure rate.

Plan for Solution: In order to fix this catastrophe for both the short and long term it is no secret we must get people working! In order to do this we need to create and bring more money and jobs to Florida; and subsequently keep them here. As we know all too well, we need more wealth coming in and less going out. So how can we accomplish this goal? Again, these are discussed in more detail in Chapters 2 and 3, however, some of the keys for this Vision for Florida jobs and economy are:

> 1.) We must protect the jobs we still have, as well as the future jobs we must create. Florida has to become a state that does much better enticing industries to relocate their facilities, jobs, and resources here. We need to successfully market

our state by aggressively promoting and upgrading our workforce and the quality of life in the Sunshine State. We must create competitive tax advantages and an overall better business environment that will bring good jobs to Florida, and keep them here for the future.

2.) Jobs, business and the economy go hand in hand, they are not separate issues. We have to do much better at creating and fostering relationships between industry employers and workers for win-win scenarios, support, and cooperation.

3.) We must clearly identify which job opportunities will be the best fit for Floridians. We cannot hit the right target if we don't know what the target is. We need to focus on present and future job opportunities and economic growth that are best aligned with Florida's workforce, environment, proprietary advantages and economic base.

4.) We need to increase the exportation of Florida's goods and services to customers in other states and foreign markets through better promotion of existing and new small business, entrepreneurship, and industry growth.

5.) We have to recognize and expand the role of education and technical schools in Florida's future economy and job success; and better integrate industry into the educational process and job placement. (See Education section below.)

6.) We need to successfully target global jobs and opportunities that could be brought to Florida, then actively entice them to relocate here. This effort should include jobs and businesses that have been outsourced or off-shored from not just the U.S., but other nations and markets as well.

7.) We must establish Florida as clearly the "best choice" state for retirement. This will bring retiree paychecks and retirement funds into the Florida economy. Their presence will increase the demand for goods and services, thus creating jobs and bolstering Florida's economic growth.

Education and Job Training

Issues: As discussed in detail in Chapter 5, Florida's education system is in dire need of serious improvement and upgrade. Florida's high school college entrance ACT (American College Testing) scores have declined four years in a row. In 2009 we ranked 47th out of 50 states in high school ACT scores with a 19.4 state average. This is clearly unacceptable. During the same four years the ACT college entry score average for admittance to Florida colleges and universities has continued to rise and is now between 23 and 29. We're going the wrong way when it comes to pre-college education. A key reason so many out of state students gain admittance to Florida universities over our own high school graduates is that they have better ACT and SAT (Scholastic Aptitude Test)

15

scores. This data is referenced in other sections and chapters of this book, and must be regarded as a critical red flag.

Plan for Solution: We must finally make meaningful upgrades to Florida's entire educational system. Our children and grandchildren's quality of life depends on it. We must be much more competitive in our scoring on standardized national college entrance exams (ACT and SAT), and quit using the FCAT (meant to measure public school performance) to justify our lack of success.

1.) We must strategically align our entire education process into a seamless system from kindergarten through graduate school and better preparing our students for today's highly competitive global economy and the future job market.

2.) We need to increase industry involvement in our education and training infrastructure, get their input and support into curriculums, and create significantly upgraded internships that prepare and introduce our students to job requirements in the workplace. Internships will help the education process to become a much larger part of the job placement process and vice-se-versa, and facilitate new graduates successfully launching their careers into the workforce.

3.) Our education curriculums have to better align with the jobs and careers of the future which will require more math, science and academic rigor. We need to place more emphasis on career fields that are high paying, less vulnerable to outsourcing, and will have the best job growth.

4.) Simply put, we require an education system that produces graduates that are motivated, educated, better prepared, and thus more competitive to enter and succeed in the workplace of tomorrow.

5.) We need to upgrade the tech and trade school image, as well as their curriculums for those who seek a career path that is not driven by a college degree; and also for those displaced workers seeking new trade and technical career fields.

Taxes and Insurance

Issues: Taxes and insurance are major expenses for virtually all Floridians. Property taxes are a major expense for most of us. Though they pay many of the bills for education and vital services provided by government, property taxes must be fair and increases should not exceed inflation or the rise in personal income.

We can't buy a home without home insurance, can't drive our cars without car insurance, and nearly all of us need health insurance to receive the medical attention we need.

Plan for Solution: A less wasteful and more efficient government is the best way to lower taxes and stop tax increases, which is discussed in Chapter 6. Although government tries to manage costs, they could take lessons from small business and industry on how to get the job done more efficiently. Less government is better than more government. Government

17

spending can be cut without sacrificing vital services. An ongoing review of government spending in order to eliminate waste as well as evaluating performance by measuring against established "best in class" benchmarks should become a more standard practice.

We should increase competition in the insurance industry by making more providers available from within and outside the state. We should ensure transparency in insurance pricing by posting rates for all types of policies and endorsements on the Department of Insurance website, providing "apples to apples" comparison pricing for consumers. It is imperative for state government to return to the business of insurance regulator, and play a less prominent role as an insurance provider at tax payer expense.

Healthcare for Floridians

Issues: The impact of escalating costs on the availability of affordable healthcare is not only a national issue, but one of particular concern here in Florida. This is discussed in more detail in Chapter 7. As Florida has a relatively large retirement population, the demand and need for quality healthcare will continue to be a top priority. The availability of resources and facilities are additionally challenged by abuse of the system such as ER visits for non-emergency situations, as well as by individuals with no health coverage including those here illegally, or are not in the tax system. We simply cannot continue to ask the tax payers to provide a free ride for those who are not contributing their fair share.

Plan for Solution: Florida needs a more strategically aligned healthcare system. We need to review how non-citizens and illegal immigrants are provided coverage at tax payer or medical provider expense, and make the necessary changes to ease the burden placed on Florida's citizens and healthcare providers. We need to better integrate and align healthcare providers (doctors, hospitals, and labs), vendors (pharmaceuticals, equipment, and supplies), payers and the legal system into a more efficient process. There should be less waste, less duplication, less unnecessary tests and procedures due to the fear of litigation, or as a requirement to get payers to provide payments to healthcare providers. We need to create a better win-win-win scenario for everyone. Additionally we need to take maximum advantage of industry resources, representatives and services to include patient assistance programs, patient aid and education materials, and medical education grants, information and funding for providers. Pharmaceutical and equipment reps can play a key role in this and need to be more utilized by healthcare providers; this will require these reps to constantly provide value and meaningful resources.

Security of Our Homes and Borders

Issues: Home foreclosures in Florida have become a tragedy of epic proportions and it is a period of our financial history that must never be repeated. Long term solutions must be implemented to minimize home foreclosures, and increase the availability to home buyers for financing and homeowner's insurance.

Security of Florida's borders is a long term problem that must be resolved fairly and effectively. This is a responsibility of the federal government, and pressure should be applied by our elected officials to better protect Floridians from illegal activities and drug trafficking. These are security issues that need serious reassessment and enforcement. Everyone living in Florida must be here legally.

Plan for Solution: The real solution to halt home foreclosures is long term economic growth and job creation. In the short term all options must be utilized more effectively to include additional refinancing scenarios, such as longer term low interest loans, as well as taking full advantage of federal programs. Property taxes that are based on inaccurate or overstated market values need to be re-evaluated and lowered. It's better for county governments to tighten their budgets than for citizens to face eviction. A more competitive homeowner's insurance environment may also help lower insurance premiums and thus lower monthly mortgages. It will require a series of efforts to keep "at risk" Floridians in their homes. Some data demonstrates that of the current homes for sale only 20% are new construction while as many as 80% are resale properties, short sales or foreclosures; this demonstrates the negative situation for the home construction industry. These are discussed in Chapters 6 and 14.

Three entry points to assist government with "Immigration and Naturalization" (INS) would include: school enrollment of students, healthcare point of service and civilian law enforcement. We need to be fair and just in resolving the issue.

Single Parent Households

Issues: As is discussed in Chapter 9, being a parent is the toughest job on the planet, and being a single parent is even tougher. Single parents all too often must perform the roles of two people. The stress and demands of competing with two income households and trying to balance work, home and kids poses tremendous challenges and responsibilities. The financial aspect is magnified for many single working mothers who are at an additional disadvantage due to disparity of wages.

Plan for Solution: Women of all ages need many avenues of support to attain the skills and credentials required to enter a career field that pays well enough to support their families. This support may include childcare, transportation, tutoring, and tuition expenses for such training. Parenting is a very serious business and everyone, both custodial and non-custodial parents, needs to be responsible in their obligations to their children, themselves and society.

Veterans

Issues: Our military veterans are our nation's heroes. They have risked life and limb to protect our way of life. We must ensure they receive the benefits they were promised without compromise. Key issues for our nation's military veterans include their pensions, healthcare and access to military bases and facilities.

Plan for Solution: This is another area where not only state government, but all elected officials from Florida must stand together as a unified voice to protect military veterans and their interests, as discussed in Chapter 10. We must keep VA hospitals and clinics, as well as all military bases, hospitals and facilities open and operating at full capacity. Pensions and retirement benefits must not be compromised. National Guard, Reserve and Active Duty veterans must all be included to receive promised benefits.

Young Professionals

Issues: Our state and nation's young professionals are our future. The unfortunate reality is that in a global economy, they must go out and compete in a very different world than the one that existed only a few decades ago. More on this is covered in Chapter 11.

Plan for Solution: We must take strong action to better prepare our young professionals for the challenges of the future. We must not burden them with a national debt they cannot pay. We must provide a business environment that creates and maintains career opportunities and high paying jobs. We must help prepare them for these opportunities and competition with a world class educational system in Florida. I believe young people need to engage in a process of lifelong learning, continue to gain knowledge about any subject or issue, develop a willingness to adapt their thinking, as well as exhibit eagerness to learn in the light of new knowledge and circumstances. I strive to do the same myself.

Senior Citizens

Issues: Senior citizen issues and interests are discussed in Chapter 12. The economic losses in the financial markets have dealt a serious setback in the value of property, equities, retirement accounts and even some pensions. This is further complicated by the increasing cost of healthcare, insurances and taxes.

Plan for Solution: We must strengthen and promote economic growth in business and industry as a partial solution to financial portfolio recovery. Additionally, we need to manage rising insurance and healthcare costs and yet provide high quality, affordable healthcare to our senior citizens.

Politics in an Election Year

As this is an election year, we will soon be inundated by campaign phone calls, TV ads, and mailers from the various candidates. Wouldn't it be nice if they focused on what they will do to move Florida forward instead of character attacks on their opponents? Getting elected to serve has too often become a battle of who can raise the most money, and wear down their opponent with insults and accusations. It's time for both parties to stop this practice. Personal attacks do not solve problems.

For us, the campaign for Governor will likely be the most widely watched race. In many ways we have missed having former Governor Jeb Bush sitting in that big chair in Tallahassee with his steady hand on the wheel. Democratic and Republican contenders will likely beat up on each other in an effort to convince the voters they are the better choice. You know the drill. One guy goes for the other guy's jugular vein to deflect any negative attention away from himself.

Didn't we play these games in grade school? Political participants need to recognize belittling their opponent does not make them a better choice nor does it improve their credentials. Let's put a stop to this nonsense and get down to business; State of Florida business. Character assassinations don't contribute to solutions, and they certainly don't add to the attacker's qualifications to perform a job.

Both parties' front runners for Governor currently hold positions on the Governor's Cabinet, which begs the question: do we want a continuation of our current situation? Should we elect either one of them to our state's highest office? Both political parties' leaders might prefer that voters don't get the opportunity to choose the candidates, they like the "good ole boys club." They may accomplish this by discouraging primary elections whenever possible. This tactic helps ensure that the same individuals with the same old tired rhetoric are elected to run our government. Is it any wonder things don't improve much? This is one reason I support some of the movements afoot such as the Tea Party.

Requests for Speaking Engagements

The subjects presented in this book are serious priorities. A great deal of material and information that could have been included is available for further study and discussion. If your group has additional interest, I will be delighted to speak for a function or gathering free of charge. Just visit my website: www.mikemccalister.com to send an email with the subject line

24

"Speaker Request." Provide an overview of the organization and/or event, number of attendees expected, location, time and date, and topic; if no topic in particular just state "The Right Future for Florida."

No doubt those whose interests or political record are challenged by this book may try to dismiss these findings. Do not be confused or misled. We will have to make a serious choice this November about who will lead Florida to "Progress and Prosperity."

If this book makes enough noise about the issues and lack of current leadership in Florida at the executive level, some who are running for office may try to discredit the information I present by making negative comments about me.

Well, let me beat them to the punch. Have I ever made anyone mad? Yes, absolutely. Have I ever done anything I wish I hadn't? Yes, absolutely. Have I ever not done something I should? Yes, absolutely. Have I ever said anything I wish I hadn't to someone? Yes, absolutely. Has anyone ever misinterpreted what I said, or misinterpreted my intentions? Yes, absolutely. Am I a saint? No, absolutely not. I am not perfect, not even close. I make mistakes, and through error I strive to improve. As Jesus said in the Gospel of John, "Let he who is without sin cast the first stone."

There, it is said. However, none of my human flaws change the issues stated in this book. The situation we face is what it is. We must RIGHT THIS SHIP!

Let there be no mistake about it my friends, we have serious challenges to overcome. Again, major issues include: job loss; recession; a failing education system; difficulties of single parent households; an aging population; and tough economic times during this new era of foreign competition. These issues can be attributed in part to the globalization and outsourcing of jobs, developing nations such as China and their industrial growth, capacity and lack of meaningful patent protection for our products, increasing costs of healthcare, immigration issues, terrorism, and the uncertainties these realities bring.

Our challenges will demand new ideas, technologies, significantly better education and job training, and the will and confidence to see this through. Just as Ronald Reagan restored America's confidence and stature during the "Cold War," we must restore Florida's confidence and stature during this "Economic War." To overcome these obstacles, we will require bold, new and energized leadership in state government that will give us real "Progress and Prosperity" for the future. Join me and together we will make things happen!

Chapter 2
Bringing Jobs and Opportunity in the Global Economy to Florida

Three Things Are Certain

In the global economy with outsourcing, off-shoring and mounting job losses, three things are certain:

1.) The global economy has changed the landscape for business, jobs and the U.S. economy, including Florida.

2.) As a state and a nation we must do a much better job of creating jobs, products and services that cannot be easily outsourced, off-shored or duplicated.

3.) The global economy is not going away; and foreign competition for jobs, products, services and customers are not going away either.

So, what caused this situation and what do we do about it? First, let's study this question for a minute, so we can identify a course of action to use to our advantage.

Having a job is extremely important. Our jobs not only give us the means, but also the self esteem and confidence to face our responsibilities. Having a job offers a certain amount of stability, the income to house and feed our families, as well as provides a launch pad for advancing our careers. There must be meaningful career jobs that will last for all who want to work.

What Caused the Global Economy?

The first step is to recognize that whether we like it, agree with it, or even want to believe it, the global economy is here to stay and we consumers helped to create it. Consumers everywhere are demanding lower priced goods and services. For businesses to be competitive, they can't pay higher costs for materials, equipment, labor, and facilities than their competition.

We refer to the entire chain of suppliers, manufacturers and distributors as the value chain. To be competitive in the global marketplace, businesses must meet consumer demands and provide goods and services of value. The word value has been defined as "meeting customer needs and expectations at the best price." Most consumers are trying to manage their money on tight budgets, and many seldom have extra money to spare. Finding the best price for goods and services has become a necessary way of life.

Other major factors fueling the global economy are the outsourcing and off-shoring of jobs. These dynamics were magnified by the emergence of developing nations with huge workforces, entering the global market place with goods and services produced with cheap labor and materials, as well as having low research and development costs (sometimes due to patent infringements).

These nations include the largest populations on the planet, with China and India representing roughly 40% of the world's people. It wasn't long before they had the resources and demand to build factories, and then progressively manufactured more complex products every year. Throw in a lack of meaningful patent protection, and these emerging nations became some of the largest makers and exporters of goods and services in the world. Keep in mind research and development (R&D) of products and labor are usually the two largest costs for any company. For that reason China has huge cost advantages over U.S. based companies. We consumers go to Walmart, buy goods made in China or Mexico, and drive them home in a foreign car. Then we wonder why we have lost jobs in this country.

Many companies based in industrialized nations such as the U.S. have had to outsource and offshore a much bigger slice of their overall operations in order to compete for customers demanding lower prices. With these changes went many U.S. based jobs. The ugly outcome is that in a global economy most consumers will not pay significantly more for products or services because of loyalty to the country of origin. Consumers are concerned about their own needs and budgets. Welcome to the free market global economy.

Jobs Lost to Outsourcing and Off-shoring, and What Is the Difference?

Differentiating outsourcing from off-shoring can be confusing, though the loss of jobs at a particular company may be a result of both. Outsourcing is the term commonly used when a particular job function has been moved outside the original organization to another organization, which is not necessarily in a foreign country. In today's highly competitive environment, this may make sense in that organizations should focus their efforts on their core business. In other words, they hire other companies to perform functions that require expertise that is outside the initial organization's core business and mission. An example would be hiring a security company for your facility. Providing guards or alarm systems would be a security company's core business. In all likelihood they could perform security duties better and more inexpensively than a company from outside their industry, as security is their specialty.

Off-shoring is different from outsourcing in that a job has been transferred by a company or even a government (believe it or not) to a different nation to be performed. Sometimes an employee of the original company will continue to do the job, but the job itself is performed in another country. We refer to this scenario as off-shored. If the company moves the job outside its own workforce and hires another company to perform the job in another country, we would say the job was outsourced and off-shored.

Industry Comparison of Job Loss and Projected Job Growth

I have chaired MBA thesis committees and taught many courses where research was done identifying jobs lost from the U.S. due to outsourcing and off shoring. It was disturbing to learn that so many lost jobs were from a number of different sectors, not just manufacturing. Some data demonstrated that administrative jobs were the most outsourced. Other industries suffering major job loss from the U.S included call center sales and service, technology related jobs, and certain executive functions.

Job growth projections may vary somewhat depending on the source of the forecast, however there is consensus that future job growth will include health care, education, and advanced technologies. Some would argue that there may be a return of manufacturing to more advanced industrialized nations such as the U.S., however the verdict is still out on this. In the manufacturing sector, high tech products likely offer the best opportunities for industrialized nations.

So What do We do Now?

First off, we must recognize that we can't just sit around and do nothing. To let the job market continue to erode is economic suicide. We need to take preventative steps to protect against more job loss. It's understood that no matter what recommendations are made, there will be winners and losers in the global job market. The key is to have more winners than losers in Florida. The logic here is undeniable. We must maximize the gains, minimize the losses, and invest wisely in preparing workers for the best future job opportunities.

Ok, so what do we do? We will use a sound methodology as demonstrated in Chapters 17 and 18 as well as the sections below.

Create More Industry Incentives to Bring Jobs to Florida

There are only so many consumers in the world, and only so many jobs required to meet the demand for goods and services at a given time. As the world works its way out of a global recession, the demand for goods and services will increase. This demand will create job growth. Where will the created jobs go? Here's the right answer: **Florida!**

This will require a serious effort to get these new jobs here, as well as keep the jobs we presently have. Companies are trying to survive and win against their competitors, so they too are looking for the best deals possible. We must acknowledge this reality, and offer companies and businesses incentives that best meet their needs and their customers' demands, versus what other states or countries might offer. These incentives must include tax advantages, a well trained and educated work force, an integrated infrastructure, a business friendly "get them here, keep them here" environment, as well as a supportive political and legal system.

Role of Small Business in Florida's Future

Small business is a significant portion of any healthy economy. Small business is the largest creator of new jobs. As a result, small business owners will be essential to economic growth in Florida. We must support and reward these businesses, and help them survive and compete.

Many times it is private entrepreneurs that bring new ideas, innovations, and technologies to the market. Excellent examples would be computer pioneers Bill Gates and Steve Jobs. We need to foster small business and more creativity and entrepreneurial spirit so as to bring "Progress and Prosperity" to the Sunshine State, so get the word of this book out there!

Chapter 3
Effective Job Training and Placement to Re-instate and Keep Displaced Florida Workers on the Job

Putting displaced workers back on the job is absolutely essential and must be done now! Unemployment benefits, temporary employment and dead end jobs are not desirable long-term solutions for Florida workers. These are short-term fixes important in our immediate time frame, but require a better, long term and sustainable replacement. I have personally experienced the hardship of losing a job because of downsizing or layoffs. Losing a job is a life jarring event. I sympathize with all those who have suffered this kind of loss.

Training Transformation

Training transformation is what many of our displaced and unemployed workers must have to secure jobs, and provide performance value in the workplace. The term "training transformation" has been used in the military and industry to describe the process of updating and upgrading the skills, knowledge, capabilities and education of a workforce.

While serving as a Colonel on Active Duty, I was assigned to represent the United States Special Operations Command on a Secretary of Defense strategic priority to research, develop and implement a Training Transformation initiative for the entire Department of Defense, affectionately known as "T2." The Executive Steering Committee (ESC) as it was called, consisted of eight to ten individuals including the Under Secretary of Defense (Personal and Readiness), either a two or three star General from each of the Active Duty Services of the Army, Marines, and Air Force, a Rear Admiral from the Navy, and myself, a Colonel representing United States Special Operations Command, which is often considered a fifth military Service.

This ESC group representing the Office of the Secretary of Defense (OSD) and all military services (DoD) was tasked to change the way the 1.5 million members of the Department of Defense trained and prepared for military operations as Joint Forces in a global and hostile environment. This was a complex multi-billion dollar program that had many moving parts, differing views, and priorities.

We identified critical gaps and shortfalls; established corrective actions; implemented better ways to educate, train, equip, prepare, deploy and integrate our military for success against current and future global threats and high-tech competition on the battle field. This program was put it into action with a comprehensive strategic implementation plan. Everyone on the ESC had key personnel to advise and assist them. For me this included among others, Colonels Paul Hand, Steve Howard and John Brainerd. Thanks guys, you were great!

We need more of a "Total Team Concept" in the civilian world here in Florida. It can and must be done. The lessons learned from T2 and similar initiatives can be utilized to facilitate the updating and upgrading of our work force capabilities, so they can compete and succeed in a highly competitive environment.

Private Job Placement

I once had a colleague who managed a private job placement and recruiting office for a national firm. He asked me to come to his facility and contact individuals with advanced professional degrees to see if they were interested in new opportunities for a business his firm represented. I attended the training program and learned to match candidates up with job opportunities. It was there that I learned this process isn't as easy one would think. In fact, it can be quite difficult. At this time more than ever before, we need to better utilize private placement firms, as state job placement cannot shoulder the enormous task of finding jobs for all unemployed Floridians alone. There needs to be more alignment and mutual cooperation between industry human resource departments, private placement firms and state job placement and training services. Additionally, better employer incentives for hiring Florida workers should be established.

A key piece of this integration requires expanding industry and employer recruiting and placement advisory groups into the high school education process. These groups would contribute input as to which skills, knowledge, expertise and behaviors businesses want from new hires. Industry requirements can then be used to develop more effective education and training curriculums that will produce competitive graduates ready for the workplace. The entire process can be taken to the next level with upgraded and expanded use of college and tech school internships. Some schools already utilize these programs, whereas others have yet to do so. It should become a more widespread practice. Again, internships present opportunities to earn college credits, gain practical job experience, provide the chance for students to prove themselves to potential employers in the workplace, and secure career field jobs.

Employers will not only impact the education, training and preparation of students, but be able to see them on the job before making hiring decisions. This can be a great win-win-win for the students, employers, and schools; yet another example of how important it is to strategically align Florida's educational system to achieve "Progress and Prosperity."

Chapter 4
Impact of Globalization and Government on Florida's Industry, Small Business and Agriculture

Much of this topic has been addressed specifically in other chapters. Yet these are critical issues, where additional discussion and reinforcement are in order. Globalization has changed the world through the level of competition, as well as the power of consumers to buy goods and services from virtually anywhere on the planet right in their own neighborhoods. Therefore the job market has changed tremendously as well, requiring more competitive training, education, preparation and performance in this global human resource pool.

We must identify the career fields and opportunities that are the best strategic fit for our workers, state and nation. In addition our state and federal governments must provide the infrastructure, environment, and assistance that create opportunities for the success of its citizens without over-regulating them.

How Can Florida Capitalize on Outsourcing?

Florida needs to better evaluate job and business opportunities that have been outsourced or off-shored, yet have the potential to be repatriated. Job and business opportunities that could be relocated to the Sunshine State must continue to be a major priority of Florida government at all levels.

The Governor's office must take the lead and be a serious facilitator, as each community will naturally prioritize their own interests first. For instance if Orlando cannot entice a manufacturer to relocate to their area because they lack port access, then perhaps Miami, Fort Lauderdale, West Palm Beach, Jacksonville, Tampa or the Panhandle can negotiate for the business. Or if unlimited hotel and convention space is needed, then Orlando may be a better choice if other cities are not as well suited. Florida cities must work together better as a team, while managing their own interests.

Small Business, Interstate and International Business

Small business and industry employers must be high priority components of the strategic plan for Florida. Everything must be on the table. Agri-business, communications, construction, defense, education, energy, healthcare, hospitality and tourism, manufacturing, transportation, insurance, among others must be involved and pursued for future sustainable economic growth. Each of these critical industries has a major presence and investment in Florida that must be protected and expanded. Additionally each of these industries faces serious individual challenges that need to be addressed.

Government oversight and regulation must be fair, consider all stakeholders, and yet help industries survive in the face of foreign investment and competition. We need growth in our economy and job base, as well as infrastructure investment. Sometimes progress brings growing pains. We need to manage any gaps that may surface during our growth phase in a way that ensures benefits outweigh disadvantages, and the outcome is a win-win scenario for all of us.

We must also do a better job of not only integrating these industries together whenever possible, but we must ensure interoperability that creates a world class economic powerhouse with sustainability here in the Sunshine State.

Florida's Growers

Agriculture is also a critical industry that must be protected. We need to find new ways to expand the sale of our agricultural products in and outside Florida. In college I majored in agriculture, and minored in earth science, so this is familiar turf for me. We have to eat as well as protect our environment; these two objectives can and must work together.

As the cover of the book states, I am a small business owner and come from an agricultural background. My grandparents owned a farm where my father was born and raised. I own and operate a small palm tree farm in Hillsborough County. I know what it's like to be out in the fields all night, doing what I can to protect my trees and praying the cold will not destroy my crop; this was a tough winter.

These experiences have shown me that we need a better crop insurance plan that requires less catastrophic loss in order to provide payments for damages. A more reasonable method to compensate growers for rehabilitation of damaged crops on their insurance claims would also help protect Florida's interests in this vital industry. Coverage from cold, insects and diseases should be included and expanded in crop insurance.

All business sectors as well as our important agriculture industry must be an integral part of this "Vision for Progress and Prosperity."

Chapter 5
Serious Improvement in Florida's Education System for Competitive Job Advantage and Our Children's Future

This chapter on education addresses another critical issue facing Florida today. In our competitive and fast paced global economy, the best jobs will most likely go to those individuals with the best education and training regardless of what state or country they may be from. References have been made in other chapters of this book to education. This chapter will build upon those references and go into greater depth.

Education Is the Key to the Future

Parents want their children and grandchildren to grow into happy, healthy and successful adults. In today's world those dreams require stronger credentials, and greater education and training than just a decade ago. It is paramount that we realize the extreme importance that emerging and developing nations such as China, Korea and India, as well as highly industrialized nations like Japan are placing on education; note the Asian culture emphasis here.

We must step up to the challenge and get better. Much better. We have some of the world's best universities, and there are many out of state and foreign students attending them. It is imperative to get Florida high school graduates better prepared for college. Only in this way will our fine universities have more Florida students attending them. According to the National Education Association Ranking of States for 2008, Florida ranks

42

last in the nation (50th) in per capita spending on education, but ranks 16th in the nation on corrections of criminals; and Florida ranks 42 out of 50 in spending on education as a percentage of total resources (Education Weekly, Quality Counts, 2009).

Author's Personal Experience

Much of my Vision and passion for Florida's educational future is a result of the education I have received, what I see in our college classrooms in Florida, what I have seen teaching college in other nations, and what I witnessed with my son's educational endeavors, particularly in high school. There are many highly qualified and dedicated teachers, administrators, support professionals and government officials working in education throughout Florida. They need to be recognized for their commitment and efforts. However they cannot address a strategic problem of this magnitude from their level. It is up to you and me, and together we can and must be the force to change it.

A few of the individuals I would like to recognize for their outstanding contributions to education include: Dr. Steve Castiglioni (Executive Director of Academic Quality Review for the largest private university in the nation), Dr. Randy Pohlman (Retired Dean of the largest private university in Florida), Dr. Patsy Kasen (Dean of Academics of a state-wide private university campus and former executive for the largest university system in the nation), and Mark Jordon, who was so motivated by the charter school concept of former Governor Jeb Bush that he started a charter elementary school, charter middle school and is working to establish a charter high school in Florida. They are but a few of the many that deserve recognition. They are not members of the Florida State University system. They are pioneers of colleges and schools that serve student needs outside government.

In order to better evaluate and develop a plan for educational improvement, it is necessary to have some first hand insight into the system at all levels. In order to do this, I serve on the Advisory Board of Directors for a charter elementary school (kindergarten through 5th grade) and as an advisor for a charter middle school (grades 6 through 8), and am working to help establish a charter high school. As previously mentioned, I have been teaching at colleges and universities (fulltime and as an adjunct) throughout the State of Florida for many years. These curriculums include undergraduate business classes, graduate and MBA classes, chairing multiple thesis committees, and serving on multiple doctoral dissertation committees.

I was also involved in developing curriculums for the Special Operations University in the education and training of U.S. Special Forces including the War on Terror. These collective experiences have provided me with meaningful insight into Florida's education from kindergarten to doctoral programs, as well as industry, national issues and interests. As a result, I also have first hand knowledge of the gaps in our educational system.

My Vision for Florida's Education

This Vision for Florida's education includes the following objectives to better strategically align and significantly improve the entire system. This book intentionally references education issues and college entrance exams in several chapters, as this is an extremely critical issue for Florida's future.

Strategically Align Florida's Entire Education System into a Seamless Organization. Florida's entire education system from kindergarten through college and graduate degree curriculums must become seamless and strategically aligned. This means that at every juncture there is a smoother transition to the next level without gaps. These junctures would include from elementary to middle school, middle school to high school, high school to college, and college to graduate school curriculums.

There should be serious reverse planning in this process. Colleges and universities must prepare graduates for the high demands in the global economy workforce. High schools need to better evaluate college requirements and skills, ensuring high school graduates are properly educated and prepared to meet these requirements. Likewise, middle schools must ensure eighth graders are ready for the higher requirements of high school curriculums; and elementary must do the same with fifth graders moving on to middle school.

Education must improve, align and integrate throughout the entire system from kindergarten through the completion of high school, and on through college and graduate programs. We need real strategic improvement.

Benchmark Florida's Education Against other States and Nations. It is important to "benchmark" by comparing ones own organization to "best in class" organizations using industry accepted performance measures. These could include: instructional school days per year, total time in school classrooms, outside the classroom study and instruction, time per day spent pursuing off-campus study, high school dropout rates and college degree completion rates. This data is readily available and should be routinely utilized for improvement.

Place Much More Focus on College Admittance Exams and Less on FCAT. National standardized college entry exams such as the ACT and SAT must take precedence over the FCAT in evaluating student progress. Colleges and universities pay little if any attention to FCAT scores that are primarily used to evaluate school performance. Instead, they want benchmark scores of nationwide standardized tests so they can evaluate and admit only the best students, no matter where they may reside. It's unfortunate that more students admitted to Florida colleges do not come from our state.

Again, Florida's ACT scores for graduating seniors in 2009 averaged 19.4, which ranked 47th out 50 states. That is the bottom 10% of the nation! During the same period the average ACT scores for students entering Florida universities has continued to increase and is now in the 23 to 29 range. Clearly Florida's educational system is not effectively preparing many of our students for college admittance; what we are doing in Florida's educational system K through 12 is not working.

I support the concept of evaluating student progress as a performance measure for teachers and schools. I would prefer that the standardized tests of ACT and SAT be an integral performance measure of this process. We cannot change the past; however, the trend of the last four years must be halted. We need to get back on track.

Better Integration of Business and Industry into Curriculum Development. This is a necessary step in order to better meet the needs and demands of the workplace. Business involvement will provide students the skills and expertise needed to gain employment in their career field, while preparing them to be job ready and able to perform to industry standards. Though some educators don't like the idea, employers offering job opportunities need to be more involved in the education and training process, as they know what they want and need in new hires. Also, we must continue to enhance curriculums with expanded areas of study in technology forecasting and development, such as more "green technologies."

Expand the Use of Internships / Externships into Job Placement. These course offerings can be the ticket for new college and tech school graduates trying to enter the workforce. As previously stated, they provide college credits, and place students in the real world work environment performing actual job responsibilities while still in college. It gives them valuable workplace experience, as well as a renewed motivation in other college classes, as they have gained first hand knowledge of the realities and competitiveness in business. These course opportunities offer students the chance to prove to potential employers that they can pick up the ball and run with it if hired. This process serves to strengthen the integration of education and training into the job market, as well as enhancing businesses' ownership in the education and job placement process.

Upgrade High School Curriculums to Include More Math and Science. Research data strongly indicates students that had tougher high school curriculums comprised of more math and science scored higher on college entrance exams, and performed better in college curriculums. As a result these students are admitted to better colleges and universities, as well as are more successful academically in college curriculums, particularly when pursuing careers in higher paying fields.

Offer More Challenges to Keep High School Students Interested in School. The high school drop-out rate in Florida is appalling and unacceptable. One study quoted by the U.S. Department of Education states only 65% of Florida pubic high school freshmen will graduate in four years as compared to 74% nationally. Many dropout students have above average abilities, but become bored and frustrated with school. I experienced this with my son, who quit high school in 11th grade. He now has a master's degree in engineering, as well as a law degree. We must develop programs to keep students interested by including additional early college coursework, and upgraded high school curriculums and internship programs that offer more challenging opportunities.

Upgrade and Elevate the Role, Credibility and Prestige of Community Colleges and Tech Schools. Many of Florida's high school students do not attend or graduate from college, yet these individuals still must enter the workforce and compete. In many other industrialized nations, high tech or specialized trade curriculums offer a meaningful alternative to college and universities. There is a good trade school educational foundation already in place in Florida. We need to upgrade their programs and curriculums so they are more attractive to high school graduates who do not intend to go on to college. Trade school programs could be better integrated into high school curriculums, to not only help keep high school students interested in school, but also to help transition them for better education, training and careers after high school.

Preschool and Early Child Development. These areas need to be more aligned with the rest of the education system. Yes, progress is being made, but early education needs to be better integrated into the statewide strategic process for education. I am not saying more government control is the answer, however I am saying better education must be a state-wide, system-wide effort.

Role of Family and Friends. We *all* must be more involved in the education system. As a single parent working multiple jobs I understand working fulltime, running a home, cooking, cleaning, and paying the bills. It is a major undertaking. However we must still be more engaged in our children's education, because the impact of our support is invaluable as they strive to learn. A better understanding of the basics at each level of education may help to explain why our entire educational system must be "seamless" from kindergarten through college.

 To keep it simple and brief, look at it like this:

Elementary: Kindergarten – 2nd grade. Establishing personal relationships with the teacher and other students, acclimating to the school environment, and learning to read.

Elementary: 3rd – 5th. Making the transition from learning basic reading skills to learning by reading.

Middle School: 6th – 8th. Moving into more specific subject matter materials and learning. Middle school teachers are more specialized in subject content such as English, math, and science teachers.

Secondary School: 9th – 12th. Courses more focused by subject matter. They may include specialty areas of study such as science classes in biology, chemistry and physics. Math courses include algebra, geometry, trigonometry and calculus.

Again, this entire system must become seamless and strategically aligned to eliminate gaps and shortfalls, putting our students on a level playing field with their competition from other states and countries for better careers and a higher quality of life. Another valuable component in the goal of preparing our students for future success is to provide role modeling and mentoring to our children at all levels. State leaders must make every effort to participate in this process.

Funding for Education

Needless to say, we have to pay for everything we do. Some will ask, "How can I advocate lower taxes, yet push for better education?" Simple. We have to do it. It is a necessity, not an option. Better education is key to our future prosperity. So, the question is *how* do we do it?

For starters, all funding lines must be more closely scrutinized. I have worked in both the public sector (government), and private sector (business and industry). I am convinced there is meaningful room for improvement in government fiscal responsibility and revenue. Areas of particular focus should include the lotto and casinos. We should examine how Nevada managed to fund many educational programs with little or no new taxes levied against their citizens. I am not saying we should encourage gambling and open additional casinos. I am saying we need to look at what we are getting from this revenue source in its present form. Is it what it should be? We need to examine other models out there, and evaluate our options. Remember, doing what we are doing now is not working if Florida students place in the bottom 10% of the country in ACT scores!

Improving Florida's education system is a cornerstone of this "Vision for Progress and Prosperity." If you agree, make some noise and get this book to everyone you know.

Chapter 6
Lower Taxes and Better Insurance Coverage for Florida

We Need Tax Incentives, Not Tax Penalties

Some believe that lowering taxes might be a bad thing to do. However, many who subscribe to this belief may not be paying higher taxes, or are not small business owners. I'll also bet they aren't managing companies struggling in a global marketplace against competitors located in a more favorable tax environment. In order to bring business and jobs to Florida, we will need to provide the same or better competitive incentives to industry and small business that they would receive elsewhere. Of course there are those who will argue if we give tax breaks our economy will suffer. How can we lose money on money that doesn't presently exist in our economy? Shouldn't we try to get 12 to15% of *something* into our tax base rather than 25 to 30% of *nothing*?

Reward Investment and Sacrifice

It is time to better reward people for obtaining higher education or training. Their efforts benefit all of us when they are able to be more competitive, make more money, and in the end pay more taxes. I would like to see tax incentives that reward success instead of penalizing it. About now our pro-tax readers are shouting that I am advocating that higher income wage earners should pay less tax than lower income wage earners. WRONG! What I am saying is those who make the sacrifice to invest in their education and training should be rewarded for their effort and investment with tax deductions for the cost of the schooling. After all, they will pay more taxes on the higher income they earn from the upgraded education and training. In some countries education is much cheaper. In the United States higher education isn't even tax deductible, unless it is required to keep your current job.

Get Everyone to Help with the Tax Burden

We need to get everyone who uses the system (healthcare, education, etc), but are not presently *in* the system (thus pay no taxes) introduced into the system to help pay for the government services they receive. Let me clarify that I'm not referring to wage earners who are in the system, but do not make enough income to pay taxes. We need to help these individuals earn more income, so they in turn will be able to help with a tax burden that must be shared.

Better Managed Government Spending at all Levels

Just like we (the taxpayers) must manage our personal finances to meet our obligations, government at all levels must do a better job of managing our tax money. Some elected officials dislike hearing us criticize their spending habits. It's time for an attitude adjustment. They are spending taxpayer funds, and must be fiscally responsible and accountable to us. Most importantly, they should remember who employs them. We voted them into office. We can just as easily vote them out.

Lower Property Taxes. Before the pro-tax folks twist my words around, let me say that we must maintain vital services, improve education, and invest in infrastructure. Now, let me also add that these things must be done without taxing people out of their homes and businesses. We shouldn't have excessive property tax increases like those sometimes experienced upon property resell or when undergoing zoning changes. There shouldn't be double-digit annual increases in government budgets, when personal income only increased 2 to 3% annually and inflation was low. We cannot afford this "luxury of government spending," or the burden it places on taxpayers.

How Do We Pay the Bills? First we need to re-evaluate all revenue streams to see if they are just and fair. Again, these include the lotto, casinos, property tax and sales tax among others. We must also maintain the current benefit of no state income tax. Next, we need to increase the tax base by adding more taxpayers, and not more tax per payer. This is a concept pro-tax supporters frequently misunderstand. We must grow Florida's economy to include:

1.) Luring business and industry to this state creating more jobs.
2.) Bringing in outside investment through relocation to Florida.
3.) Enticing retirees to relocate and bring their financial resources to our state.
4.) Creating more small business in Florida.
5.) Improving worker education providing a human resource pool that Florida and businesses from other states demand. Let's be the leading

"In-sourcer of Jobs."

6)   Creating a higher demand for more exportation of Florida products and services to other states and nations.

Additionally, we should investigate other creative ways to pay the bills for state business. The point is we need to do it without increasing the tax burden on Florida's citizens and businesses. We need government to get better, not bigger.

Better Property Insurance Coverage for Floridians

This chapter may get a response from insurance companies. The fact is Floridians need affordable and dependable insurance coverage for their homes, vehicles and businesses. (We will address health insurance in Chapter 7.) We need to provide a way for insurance companies to better manage their risks, and maintain the financial means to pay claims while providing Floridians with needed coverage at fair prices. This plan for Florida includes creating a more competitive environment for insurance coverage in the Sunshine State. This scenario will offer consumers and businesses more and better choices for coverage while working to get state government out of the insurance business.

This is a serious problem that must be resolved. It is incredibly stressful to worry if your homeowner's insurance will be cancelled, or to scramble to try and obtain a reasonable new policy if it is terminated. It is virtually impossible to obtain a home loan without having insurance on the property. When I purchased my current residence a few years ago, I couldn't get homeowner's coverage from the company that covered my car. The insurance company told me the new home was in Hillsborough County which presented a "coastal risk," but they would have given me the needed coverage if I already had a current homeowner's policy with them. Since I was living in a rental home, that was a dead end. I pointed out that the property is over twenty miles from the coast, but that didn't sway them either. My frustration was significantly elevated when I asked the seller of the home I was buying who his insurance was with. Guess what? It was my auto insurance company. When I informed the insurance company that they already covered the property in question, I was then told no new policies were being written in any coastal counties regardless how far they were located from water.

For most of us, our home is our sanctuary and biggest financial investment. It is usually our largest equity position, with much of our life's savings and hard work invested in it. Clearly to properly protect our homes we need a much better system.

Vehicle Insurance

Vehicle insurance is another critical issue. It is unwise and illegal to operate a licensed motor vehicle on public roads in Florida without vehicle insurance. However as with homeowner's coverage, we are at the mercy of insurers. Since insurance providers assume much of the risk for our actions when we are behind the wheel, we must limit their exposure by being responsible drivers.

Regulators must ensure that Floridians are receiving the coverage limits they need, at prices that are fair, competitive and affordable. This includes the means for quicker and easier pricing to evaluate equivalent coverage, such as the posting of policy prices on a state website with apples to apples and oranges to oranges comparisons.

This "Vision for Progress and Prosperity" includes the need for lower taxes and better insurance for Floridians. If you agree then get the word of this book out!

Chapter 7

Affordable Healthcare That Serves the Needs of Floridians

With all the debate about healthcare taking place at the federal level, what else remains to be said on the subject? How about this: we need affordable, available, high quality health care for Floridians. As with the methodology we have discussed in previous chapters, Florida needs to better strategically align the entire healthcare system. It must include all critical components and participants including:

Providers: Doctors, hospitals, labs & testing facilities

Payers: Managed care and insurance companies, Medicaid, Medicare, Veterans Administration, Department of Defense, and uninsured citizens

Vendors: Pharmaceutical, biotechnology, device and equipment companies

Others: Disposables, etc.

It is obvious that integrating and aligning these stakeholders into a more efficient and affordable Florida health care system will be a very difficult task as each of these participants may have differing or opposing objectives. However it must be done. To do so will require better give and take from all participants. It will also require better management, as well as less duplication, waste, and unnecessary procedures throughout the system.

Publicly Held Healthcare Companies

As much as we may not like it, certain facts must be faced. Publicly held companies such as many for profit hospitals, pharmaceutical companies and managed care companies are overseen by Securities and Exchange Commission (SEC).

The SEC is a government agency created by Congress who is tasked to ensure publicly held companies are managed in a way that protects the interests of stockholders (many of whom are us). Our 401K plans, mutual funds and stock portfolios are dependent on publicly held companies not only surviving, but making a profit. Decreased profits for companies often lead to decreased jobs and job loss. And the harsh reality is if a publicly held company lowers its profitability too much, the Board of Directors will likely fire the existing management and hire a new team tasked to increase profits for stockholders. Talk about a dual edged sword. People not only want their investments to pay off, but they also want increased job growth; this at the same time they need cheaper costs in all economic sectors including healthcare.

Industry Experience

For many years I have worked with doctors, pharmacists, hospitals and payers as a vendor in the healthcare industry. I've held positions in training, marketing and contracting products to hospitals, pharmacies, the federal government (VA & DoD) and managed care payers. I have worked with every major medical school and teaching hospital in Florida, and literally hundreds of doctors throughout the Sunshine State from Pensacola to Miami.

I have worked closely with patient support groups and patient advocates. I have been with a physician many times when a patient is diagnosed with a life-threatening disease, worked to get the patient enrolled in a national disease state registry, coordinated the process of getting the prescribed treatment approved by the payer, contacted a specialty pharmacy, and had the medication delivered directly to the patient or physician. At times I have obtained very expensive medications for patients free of charge through compassionate use programs. I have tried to be a part of the solution from the inside, not just complain about it from the outside.

Prescription Drugs

Let me say this before critics of this book bring it up. Yes, I have worked for pharmaceutical companies. Yes, prescription drugs are too expensive. Yes, pharmaceutical companies are making profits. And yes, I want cheaper drugs too! I have a reputation in the industry of occasionally disagreeing with my superiors, taking the side of the doctors, hospitals and patients. On a few occasions, I chose to walk away, taking the high road rather than remaining in their employ.

Now let's look at some things you aren't being told. Pharmaceutical companies spend a great deal of their stockholder's money researching and developing drugs to bring to market to meet patient needs. No one else is going to do this, and we need it to advance the treatment of disease.

Many countries have lax laws that allow the breach of patents, therefore robbing companies and stockholders of a return on their investment, which again may be in your portfolio, the same portfolio you need to grow for retirement.

And what about importing drugs from Canada, and other nations? First of all, the drugs from foreign countries are likely made by the same pharmaceutical companies that make and sell them here in the U.S. One of the reasons drugs are so expensive in our country is because of the cost of getting a drug approved by the FDA so it can be prescribed, distributed and used here. Some estimations are that it costs as much as a billion dollars to research, develop, gain FDA approval and bring a drug to market for use in the U.S. Where does this money come from? It comes from the drug company, which again may be owned by you in your portfolio or 401K plan. Do you think a company will spend a billion dollars for a drug approval for use in the U.S. if they can't recover the costs? Of course not.

Do you think that a pharmaceutical company will sell enough of a pharmaceutical prescription drug to Canada, a country with 35 million people, at a reduced cost (because they have less expensive approval processes) for them to resell it to the U.S., a country with 350 million people, thus bypassing recovery costs of bringing the drug to market in the U.S.? Nope. Not hardly! Can the FDA assure all offshore drugs are safe and effective? No, they cannot. Some data indicates that an alarming amount of off-shore drugs purchased on-line by U.S. consumers looking for lower priced prescription drugs are counterfeit. Some bargain huh? After all, it is much easier to make phony pills than phony money. Think about it.

A few comments should be made about generic drugs. Not everyone understands that generic drugs are only available for pharmaceutical products that have expired patent protection. Again, with the cost of bringing new drugs to market, which often takes five to ten years (sometimes longer), pharmaceutical companies will not spend their stockholders money to research, develop and get drug approval if they cannot recover these costs. Generic pharmaceutical companies often do not do research or develop new drugs; thus they incur less costs in selling a product. Generic companies therefore, are unlikely to provide the medical communities with new treatment options. Without the research pharmaceutical companies investing major resources of their stockholders equity in new drug development, we would only have old products. This is particularly scary in treating infectious diseases and orphan diseases for which there may be no treatments available. This is why patent protection is important and why countries that ignore patents are a serious threat to U.S. companies and their investments, in pharmaceuticals as well as other technologies and products. We need generic prescription drugs to treat many diseases cheaply, and brand name prescription drugs to treat diseases which require new products.

The fact is none of these issues are as easy as we have often been led to believe. But it makes for great TV, and political drama. What is needed is real and total transparency of the whole picture, so we can actually see the roots of the problems that exist, better understand them, and then pursue equitable solutions.

Aligning Healthcare

There are actions that would help cut healthcare costs, and some of them need to be implemented. Ok, whose job is that? Exactly! Again, this is why we need to better align all stakeholders and participants to eliminate waste, duplication and unnecessary tests because a provider is afraid of malpractice suits or not receiving reimbursement for services. Administrative costs can be reduced through better technology.

After twenty five years in this industry I am convinced of the following:

1.) We can't afford NOT to have affordable, available, high quality health care.

2.) We must continue to increase public awareness about healthier lifestyles, and reward those who practice them. Our bodies are incredible machines, but they require the appropriate maintenance, including good nutrition and proper exercise. A healthier lifestyle for our citizens needs to be a key component of any plan to lower health care costs, but in a way that rewards us for doing so. In truth we all know there are things we can and cannot control. We must focus on those within our control, and do what is best for each of us individually. This may require losing a few pounds, more exercise, less fat in our diets, etc. Is there really anything to argue about here?

Possible tax incentives for gym memberships might be a good place to start. Some may attack this recommendation, claiming I am for mandatory lifestyles. Well, if telling you we'll all have less health care costs, as well as saving money while looking, and feeling better is a bad idea, then let them say it. I bet your doctor agrees with me. Many car manufacturers started including free oil changes with their warranties. This move helped ensure that cars sold were properly maintained, thus lowering the cost of warranty repairs. That's just good business. The same reasoning should be applied when it comes to caring for our bodies. We need better body maintenance.

3.) Physicians face huge professional and financial risks, particularly when treating patients that develop complications or are suffering from very difficult to treat conditions. Their careers shouldn't be on the line for treating higher risk patients. It takes years to become a doctor, and many accumulate huge financial debts that come due at the end of their educational process. They face mounting fears of lawsuits, higher insurance premiums, as well as reimbursement difficulties from payers; all of these factors can lead to the ordering of additional testing for patients, and increasing the cost of care. One recent trend is that more physicians desire to be employed by hospitals or clinics versus being in a private independent practice. They have concerns that with healthcare reform, that hospitals may be the recipients of global payments by government. Some doctors fear that if they are not aligned now with hospital providers, they may be at a financial disadvantage.

4.) Hospitals face mounting problems as well. They must provide an infrastructure for doctors to treat patients. Yet many times physicians are not hospital employees, they may only have admitting privileges. In this case physicians are credentialed by the hospital Med-Exec Committee to perform specified procedures in the hospital, and must bear the cost of their own malpractice insurance. (This is usually different in a teaching hospital aligned with a medical school.) Hospitals are required to receive, manage, service and discharge almost anyone who shows up at their ER door. They too have huge risk issues, must perform required medical care (service intensity) for patients on the amount of money a payer provides them for each particular patient's illness or injury (referred to as a Diagnosis Related Group or DRG); yet still meet quality of care standards from the doctors (admitters), state authorities, JCAHO (the Joint Commission, formerly the Joint Commission on Accreditation of Healthcare Organizations) as well as their patients. They must pay virtually all costs of treatment (except doctor fees) including drugs, personnel, lab, implants, etc. out of the fixed amount provided by the payer. If the length of stay in the hospital or other associated costs to treat the patient exceeds the amount the payer is obligated to submit, the hospital has to absorb the loss. In the case of the uninsured and illegal immigrants, hospitals may have to absorb their healthcare costs without payment for service. How often do we see a grocery store give away free food or a car dealer give free cars to people who can't afford them? Hospitals have bills to pay too.

5.) There should be better partnering between industry vendors and providers such as hospitals, physicians and medical centers; meeting goals, objectives and bringing benefit to all. Valid pharmacoeconomic data should be reviewed by all providers and vendors that may factually offer a total treatment savings through decreased length of stay, better outcomes, lowered risk or cost avoidance. Vendors may have the means to offer unsolicited educational grants and continuing education speaker programs to hospitals, physicians, medical schools and centers; these do have to comply with all provider, vendor, ACCME, and PHARMA guidelines. They may be able to offer better pricing on pharmaceuticals and related products. Better vendor access with healthcare professionals and providers could provide better service from industry to providers and would be beneficial. Pharmaceutical reps (there are hundreds of them from Pensacola to Miami) may have access to company resources that are going to be utilized somewhere in the U.S. We should tap into those resources for use here in Florida whenever possible and appropriate. To do so will require better communication and partnering of vendors with hospitals, physicians and other healthcare providers. Let me say to those who are concerned that vendors will have influence over the products that are purchased; the medical community is likely already buying from them or their competitors, and there are guidelines that address this issue that must be followed. I am talking about a value added approach, not cost added. There can be lost opportunities when the medical industry is denied access to providers. This is not smart business. We are looking for cost savings right? Obtaining savings or vendor resources may require providers to more routinely set aside time to meet with industry, and use these contacts to their advantage, as it can provide benefit. Again, gaining access to healthcare providers is a major expense for vendors and in the end adds to the price of products and pharmaceuticals. Likewise vendors must not waste the hospital's or provider's time, must operate within hospital or clinic access guidelines and must provide high quality information, educational services, patient materials and/or credible treatment options with real value and/or cost savings. Better access through expanded Noon Conferences, Grand Rounds, etc. in which physicians are encouraged to interact with vendors are potential options. Pharmaceutical reps also may provide patient medication samples which by law (Prescription Drug Marketing Act) requires interactions with the physicians; or other saving alternatives such as patient assistance programs or vouchers to help with the cost of drugs. According to a study done by Joseph Barfett and published in the McGill Journal of Medicine (2004) pharmaceutical companies spent $21 billion dollars marketing pharmaceuticals in the U.S. in

2002, and 56% of this was for samples and vouchers. We should ensure Floridians benefit as much as possible from these programs. All parties should be open and more willing to work together for better services, products and decreased cost and waste throughout the system. I once accepted a pharmaceutical position because the company offered their brand name drugs to hospitals at the same cost as generics, while providing value added benefits. Yet, there were still facilities that would not make time to hear about these advantages. We all need to work together better to improve our healthcare system, period.

6.) Malpractice and risk insurance for Florida's doctors and hospitals must be available and competitively priced. A number of doctors have left the state, and some doctors and hospitals are eliminating certain services as a result of this issue. Some recent data may suggest the cost of healthcare due to malpractice has leveled off; however the verdict is still out on this. When doctors and hospitals have to practice defensive medicine with unnecessary tests or procedures to avoid lawsuits it adds to the bottom line costs for everyone concerned.

7.) More emphasis should be placed on primary care. The practice of patients going to hospital ERs for non-emergency treatment needs to be discouraged. Emergency rooms are often the most expensive way to treat non-emergency conditions, and this practice can place an unnecessary burden on hospitals and payers, be they public or private. Likewise, government needs to look for reimbursement processes that allow patients on government programs such as Medicare, or Medicaid to receive treatment options in less expensive modalities than those requiring hospital admittance to receive coverage of benefits or reimbursement.

8.) Healthcare providers are required to stay current in their field to maintain licensing and continuing medical education (CME) requirements. Vendors can often provide recent and valuable information on treatment options and may be able to assist with the cost of educational programs. Many healthcare professionals seek additional training in new treatment options, as well as additional education and degrees. I have taught university MBA classes at hospitals for executives, physicians, nurses, techs, and pharmacists throughout Florida. In these classes we strive to teach better business management, cost analysis, operations and systems management as well as performance measures. I would applaud and encourage more hospital executives continue advancing their education. There are numerous ways to cut costs throughout the healthcare system. They must be identified and implemented. Progress is being made, but more is needed.

9.) Government run health care is not the answer to our healthcare problems. Any government program that does not have a majority of public support should not be forced upon the public at tax payer expense.

10.) An area that may be in need of additional attention for the civilian healthcare community is awareness, preparedness and treatment training of casualties in case of a terrorist attack against Americans on U.S. soil. No one likes to think about this issue, however public knowledge of our preparedness may provide a deterrent to those who would do us harm. If our adversaries know we are ready, it takes away much of their motivation.

Recognizing Dedicated Healthcare Professionals

Recognition is given here to the contribution of the many disease state support groups that have formed throughout Florida. They provide each other and their families important information and support during these difficult times.

Again, we are fortunate to have the many dedicated, hardworking and exceptional healthcare providers we have in Florida. These doctors, nurses, hospitals, pharmacists, techs and support personnel are our key to a long and high quality of life and we thank you for your commitments, sacrifices and service. You are the best the world has to offer and I am proud to have been associated with you!

Strategic alignment of Florida's healthcare system is another important component of this "Vision for Progress and Prosperity."

Chapter 8
Family, Community and State. What More Can We Do?

Family

I was blessed to have had the privilege of raising a son. Attending PTA meetings and school events, enjoying watching him become an Eagle Scout and receive the God & Country Award (as I did at his age), taking karate class together; these were all milestones in our lives. I would not have wanted to miss any special times and memories with my child.

There were dark days though, such as the time when he and his high school principal disagreed on some issues, so he decided to skip his junior and senior years of high school to work at a fast food restaurant. I was hoping someone would step up and be the adult in that situation. No such luck. As a result, I was thoroughly disgusted with both of them. This is one of the reasons that I believe we have to offer greater challenges for young people in the first twelve years of school so they will feel *compelled* to graduate.

After mastering the art of flipping burgers, the lights came back on and my son went to St. Petersburg College. There he became a math tutor and went on to graduate from the University of South Florida College of Engineering in Tampa. I was tremendously relieved to see him finally realize his lifelong dream of becoming an engineer. It was also a great day in my family when my parents attended my son's graduation from law school at the University of Florida in Gainesville. They were so proud, and it was wonderful to see them honored by his success.

Community

Volunteerism is an essential element in any community. I've always believed in giving back, whether it was serving at my son's school, working with the Boy Scouts, being an intramural football coach, or donating time and/or resources to community causes. There are very worthy organizations that provide the structure for citizens to get involved and contribute to issues important to them. These include among others: donating blood through the Red Cross; assisting in disaster relief, Christmas charities, senior citizen services or rehabilitation programs through the Salvation Army; supporting the United Way's efforts in education, income stability and health; promoting a strong national security through the American Legion or VFW; or helping the Humane Society and the SPCA lead the fight against animal cruelty. Many of you are active in your own communities; your contributions and service are needed and applauded.

I would like to see greater recognition from elected leaders for the everyday citizen who actively volunteers his or her talents to their community. I once heard a statement that said "bestowing awards says almost as much about those who recognize and honor a good deed as the recipient."

This is an area in which the military community seems to excel. I think back to the times when on separate occasions I received the Missouri

Meritorious Service Medal for Merit, and the Missouri Conspicuous Service Medal for Valor, both given by the Governor of Missouri. These were great honors for me, but even more importantly it brought recognition to the military unit, the people with which I served at the time, as well as my community. Recognizing the good in people can be a very positive thing.

On another occasion, I was awarded the Valley Forge Cross for Heroism by the National Guard Association of the United States for saving a woman who was trapped and drowning in a submerged vehicle during a rainstorm. This too brought public recognition to the National Guard in my community and the value of the training they provide. The episode was a life-changing event for me as well, as it was the victim's horrified daughter who gave me the courage to face disaster and take quick action. I will never forget the terrified look in her eyes as she said "I killed my mom."

The daughter was driving the car when it went out of control, overturned, and landed upside down beneath the water in a flooded stream. Fortunately she had been thrown clear and was unharmed except for some disorientation. Her mother was a different story entirely. I pulled her out of the water with the help of another motorist. She was blue and cold with no pulse. After administering CPR for what seemed an eternity, she expelled a large volume of dirty water and began shivering. I was then able to get her breathing again, and by the time the ambulance arrived she was talking. Because the victim appeared completely lifeless, I would

74

have given up after a couple minutes, had her daughter not given me the strength and determination to continue. The tears of joy that ran down the daughter's cheeks as she hugged her mother were all the thanks I needed.

I thought about how that could have been my parent or my son. It reminded me how precious and fleeting life can be, and how important it is to do what we can when a crisis faces us. We must look after one another, and rise to the occasion when the time comes.

Perhaps the most rewarding community experience I participated in was during the historic flooding of small rural Missouri towns along the Mississippi River in late 1982 into early 1983. At the time I was the Commanding Officer of a Combat Engineer Company in the National Guard. People were being forced from their businesses and homes by rising water, which in the case of a major river can be extremely treacherous.

The Governor declared a state of emergency, and called my Guard unit into action on "State Emergency Duty." I will never forget how the look of fear and despair on those cold, hungry faces changed to smiles of relief when we rolled in with bulldozers, back hoes, front end loaders, road graders, and five ton dump trucks loaded with supplies, food and drinking water; all manned by uniformed National Guardsmen. When we started repairing breached levees, sandbagging homes, and redirecting floodwaters they pitched in too. Hand in hand we worked around the clock for many days to save their homes and towns. They knew much work lay ahead, but they also knew they were not alone in the task. We became a community that displayed strength in numbers.

In recognition of our successful efforts the Office of the Secretary of Defense (OSD) awarded my unit the Humanitarian Service Medal; the first time in history a National Guard or Reserve unit had ever received this award.

Our citizens provide valuable assistance and resources to people of all ages and genders who may be going through the most difficult of times in their lives. A number of volunteer organizations provide the essentials of food, clothing, shelter as well as ongoing individual group empowerment support and care, in addition to employment skills, and legal assistance. Recognition is given to the role and value that these groups provide to those suffering from life altering events, diseases and injuries. Without the help of those who care, many individuals would slip through the cracks and never experience the fullness of life. I applaud those who tirelessly work to help make the world around them a better place.

I would also like to recognize the work done by community animal activists, who donate time and money to assist displaced and neglected pets and wildlife. Animal activists step up to the plate again and again, showing passion, concern and dedication for their cause. It is an issue important to me as well. On many occasions I have taken lost and homeless animals to my veterinarian for treatment, and later worked to find homes for them.

As is discussed in Chapter 15, I recognize the importance of good stewardship and protecting Florida's environment for future generations. In this regard recognition goes to those individuals, groups and organizations working to protect our natural resources.

Community cohesiveness is a major part of this Vision for Florida, from the Governor's office down to every citizen. We owe a great debt to the many civic organizations that provide support and services to our communities in almost all facets of life. We are all in this together.

State

This brings us to the question of what can and must we do to move Florida forward. Well, again, it is up to us. Get more involved in choosing your leaders and elected officials. You are the hiring and firing authority. Choosing the right leaders is an incredibly important job.

We must get serious and progress past the point of going to vote and pushing the button by a name, simply because we have read it on a bumper sticker. You've heard of Osama bin Laden. Would you vote for him? Of course not. Voting should be like picking a college for your kids, or choosing investments. Voting should be based on research and thought, not just advertising.

It is a shame that the parties and political analysts are convinced that the only candidates worth backing are those who raise the most money and have political party support and clout. Haven't we had enough of this "elitism?" We need leaders who live outside their political ambitions. It is up to us to select and hire these leaders. We need to know why we should entrust our future to the selected candidates. What are their plans if elected? Do they really understand our concerns, or do they just tell us what we want to hear? Will they really put themselves on the line for us? Can we trust them? Have they walked in your shoes?

We must demand that our political parties have meaningful primary elections that begin with allowing *us* to choose our candidates. Primaries are our only real opportunity to vote for candidates of our own choosing. We should not be force fed choices made by some political party leaders.

Finally, if any of your friends, family or colleagues has unique leadership skills, and/or experiences, encourage them to run for office. Get involved. Make the commitment to help them make a difference. Help them get the word out. Elected officials must be made of more substance than the amount of money they raise and subsequently spend on getting your vote.

Electing the right leaders to run our state is paramount to this "Vision for Progress and Prosperity."

Chapter 9
Single Parents: Challenges at Home and Work

Parenting: The Toughest Job on the Planet!

Well my fellow single parents, here we are. This is our chapter, and we must have a serious say about the future of this state. According to the Anne E. Casey Foundation in 2009 (Kids Count Data Book), Florida ranks 43rd in the nation with 36% of our children living in single parent households. I became a single custodial parent of a four-year-old son, who lived with me through his college years, until he went to law school. He is the pride of my life, and my greatest contribution. Watching him grow gave me the will, determination and toughness to endure days when it would have been easier to give up. He was a trooper, living through job relocations and military duty moves.

In parenting we sometimes experience times of great anxiety and fear over the well being and health of our children. My greatest scare came when my son was three years old and developed a serious infection that required hospitalization. None of the medications available were working, and his concerned doctors informed us there may not be a successful solution. That kind of news quickly moves all other issues you previously thought were important to the back burner. Fortunately his doctors eventually found medications that worked, and my son fully recovered.

There were many times over the years that I knew the Lord was looking out for me my son through difficult days, and the single set of footprints in the sand were indeed the times when He was carrying me!

Recognizing Moms

The majority of single parent households are managed by women. These moms carry huge responsibilities alone. They regularly juggle more tasks than a circus performer who pedals a bike with six pins in the air. Florida could not function without the contributions and sacrifices you make day in and day out. Ladies, take a bow, you've earned it!

Paying the Bills

Having been a single parent for over twenty years, I know the stress and pressure of being the only bill payer in the house. We compete in nearly every way with two income households, but manage on a one income budget. Single women may find this particularly frustrating, as their wages are often a great deal lower than male counterparts performing the same duties. Job loss by a non-custodial parent who is then less able to make child support payments to the custodial parent adds an additional financial hardship. Worst of all is when there is little or no financial support from an irresponsible non-custodial parent. For the sake of the children that the financial support was meant to benefit, our judicial system needs to be more responsive in enforcing child support delinquencies.

Like many of you, I know what it is like to work multiple jobs to provide for my child. I taught college at night and on weekends in addition to my day job. Even households with two employed adults are struggling to make ends meet these days. Many of you deserve to be awarded an "Honorary Doctorate in Finance" for making it work. I was fortunate that my former wife took an active interest in my son's life and well-being. We often did things together to make his life as normal as possible, while still living our separate lives. Thank you Debbie, we did it.

Jobs, Careers and the Workplace

Many studies demonstrate with solid quantitative data that single parent households have become a large sector of our society and workplace. We are neighbors, workers, supervisors and executives in America's business world. With that being said, there are still many challenges and difficulties for single parents. Two that have major impact are scheduling (time conflicts) and setting priorities.

I remember when my son was small, I had a travel job. I was very grateful to have found a day care center that opened at 6 AM, and took the children to kindergarten. However, if I was five minutes late picking him up at 6 PM, they were waiting for me with a lynch mob. Understandably they too had responsibilities and needed to leave. A better plan is needed for this scenario. When I traveled overnight, I was fortunate to have day care centers in those towns as well. This allowed me to take my son with me.

You name it, I had to learn it. Dad duties can be tough until one gets the hang of it. I was a volunteer taxi driver, Boy Scout Leader, football coach, karate student and hockey parent. You know the drill. Even households with two working parents face these challenges. And of course the helping with homework, which is very important. It would be nice though if our kids would not wait until 9 pm to tell us they have a science project or a book report due the next day. I think you get the picture.

When my four-year-old son came to live with me, my boss said he hoped that parenting duties wouldn't have an effect on my job. I asked him if he was kidding. A four-year-old child had just moved in with his single father, depending on me for everything, and this guy hoped it wouldn't affect me? I reminded him that my child was the main reason I worked at that job, and he was my top priority in life. I also pointed out that I did not have a stay at home spouse like he did, and that I was probably a more committed employee because I was the only breadwinner in our home. We got it worked out, but not before I considered "calling in an air strike" on his office.

Progress is being made to better accommodate the needs and challenges facing single parent professionals, but there is still more to be done. Hiring decisions, promotion selections, as well as other opportunities in the workplace must continue to be equally available to all workers regardless of their parental responsibilities.

Relationships

Having been single for many years, I also had relationships with other single parents, including dating. This is supposed to be fun, right? Let's see here: your kids, my kids; your ex, my ex; your family and friends, my family and friends; your job and my job. The whole process sometimes made a root canal sound pretty good. I also learned a whole new meaning for the dating term "recycle"; when you go back and try it again with someone only to remember five minutes into the date why it didn't work out before. Well, we are who we are, and we're all trying. I have met many good people, and have learned lessons along my dating journey that helped me become a better parent and person. Thanks again ladies! There is a common bond among single parents, and it provides us with a support group framework. What would we do without the family and friends that make up this part of our lives?

Our Children's and Family's Future

We must continue to be a force because we are raising our nation's future. Children of single working parents may have less money, and fewer expensive clothes and toys. But they are learning serious survival skills that will serve them well later in life. They will never forget the nurturing, love, and sacrifices you made for them as they matured. Being a single working parent is a badge of honor. Wear it proudly! Parenting will play a major role in this "Vision for Progress and Prosperity."

Chapter 10
Veterans: Fulfilling the Commitment to Our Nation's Heroes

This chapter has special meaning for me. In the thirty five years I have spent earning a living, some of the best and brightest individuals I have ever worked with were the men and women of the United States military. These heroes represent the very best of who and what we are; they are the essence of our soul as a free nation, and are second to none.

Like many of you, I come from a military family. My dad, Eugene McCalister, was one of three brothers, all of whom served in World War II. He was in the European theater on a ship in the Mediterranean. His older brother, LeRoy McCalister, was a Marine who received three Purple Hearts for three island invasions in the Pacific. His oldest brother, Buster McCalister, was killed aboard the battleship USS South Dakota during the Battle of Guadalcanal, and buried at sea. The American Legion Post in Farmington, MO is named after Buster in his honor. Additionally, my grandfather,
William McCalister served in the Army during WW I under the command of Harry S. Truman.

Veterans Benefits Must Be Protected!

Ok, let's get straight to it! Without any doubt the political leadership in Florida must simply do whatever it takes to ensure that military veterans living in Florida receive everything they earned and were promised. Period! There can be no compromise, no un-kept promises. Florida's military veterans put their lives on the line to protect our way of life. The world owes these heroes and their families a huge debt of gratitude, and they are entitled to the retirements, pensions, healthcare, military base support and amenities they earned.

Again, these entitlements must include the following and more:

1.) Access to high quality healthcare at military bases, military and civilian hospitals, clinics, pharmacies and dental services.

2.) Access to VA hospitals and facilities without long waits.

3.) Payments of pensions, retirements and disability.

4.) Access to military bases, commissaries, facilities. NO BASE CLOSURES!

5.) All National Guard and Reserve Units must remain intact and operational, with facilities manned and functioning.

6.) Effective job and home protection for mobilized Reservists and Guard members at the national and state levels. (This is more important than ever before.)

Military Service

Like most veterans, some of the proudest moments of my life came while wearing the military uniform of our great nation. It is the feeling of knowing you are a part of something much bigger and more important than yourself. The camaraderie and associations made in the military remain with soldiers, sailors, airmen and marines all their lives.

For this soldier, I was fortunate enough to serve for over thirty years in the ranks from Private E-1 to full Colonel. I wouldn't give up the memories of basic combat training in Fort Jackson in February, being commissioned a 2nd LT, or making 1st LT and getting rid of that "butter bar" for anything. I was fortunate enough to have served in the Florida National Guard, the Army Reserve, and as an Active Duty Colonel at the United States Special Operations Command in the Center for Operations, Plans and Policy where I had the honor to contribute in the War against Terror.

As mentioned earlier in the book, during this assignment I was involved in highly classified operations, co-authored reports on base closures (BRAC), infrastructure investment recommendations, served as lead investigator of a global study and was the subject matter expert at a Congressional testimony before the U.S. Congressional Committee on Government Reform. This global study resulted in the allocation of additional resources to Special Forces war fighters in the War on Terror.

Today's Military

Many of those who have never worn a military uniform or don't have close family or friends in the military have very little first-hand knowledge of how fine our young soldiers, marines, airmen and sailors really are. I cannot express how much I miss being part of such an elite organization. Compared to the corporate world, a military environment is extremely team oriented, mission driven, and community sponsored.

When I was completing the War College as a Lieutenant Colonel, we studied and learned the concepts and processes of establishing U.S vital interests, national objectives and developing a global security strategy and policy. We evaluated global forces, threats, and competition, and created a military force structure with war plans and resources that ensured our capability to protect our nation's interests and way of life.

While serving as a Colonel on Active Duty following the 9/11 Terrorist Attacks, I was fortunate to be involved in the strategic process; involved first hand with the incredible talent, decision making and execution of a Unified and Joint Command at the Four Star General level in planning, evaluating, implementing, executing and winning on the battlefield. These men and women are good. Really good! I learned here, more than ever before, to identify every issue, risk, factor, capability, trend, strength, weakness, opportunity, the competition, and the development and execution of strategy and tactics to ensure victory.

Individuals Acknowledged and Saluted

Though they may not like the recognition, I must at least briefly acknowledge some of the key figures and mentors I had in my military career:

1.) SFC Pena, my basic training Drill Instructor who welcomed me to Fort Jackson in the "front lean & rest position," taught me "my left from my right" and "to get my head out." They were good lessons for an eighteen year old and I will not forget you Drill Sergeant.

2.) Lt Colonel Jerry Stone, my Company Commander who sent me to OCS.

3.) CSM Paul Summers, who taught me about the troops, and what they expect in a leader.

4.) Colonel David Moll, my Battalion and Group Commander who taught me how to be a military combat arms officer.

5.) Colonel Steve Howard, a career Active Duty Air Force officer and my right hand man at USSOCOM who "had my six" during high tempo times.

6.) Colonel Paul Hand, a career Active Duty Marine and my boss at USSOCOM who taught me how to "put on and wear the Eagles" and how to be an Active Duty Colonel.

7.) Major General Geoffrey Lambert, a career Active Duty General, and the Director for Operations at USSOCOM who taught me Global Operations in the War on Terror.

8.) Four-Star General Doug Brown, a career Active Duty General and former Commander of USSOCOM and all Special Operations Forces world-wide, who was my senior rater, teaching me about the political nature of the Military-industrial complex and leadership at the top.

Thank you gentlemen. You meant more to me than you will ever know, and your contributions to our nation are greater than the public will ever comprehend. I salute you!

Ensuring that the interests of our nation's Veterans are protected is a non-wavering aspect of this "Vision for Progress and Prosperity."

Chapter 11

Young Professionals: The Future of Florida and the USA

You Are the Future!

Ok young professionals, put your hands on the wheel and become a force to be reckoned with! The time is now to upgrade and utilize the education, training, experience, initiative and desire you have to move your professional life forward and keep it progressing throughout your career.

Soon my generation will begin turning the controls over to you. We must make this transition together. To successfully accomplish this task, my generation must establish an environment that provides you with the tools and opportunities needed. In turn, you must be ready to run with the ball. So, how do we make this happen?

Don't Be Overly Stressed. You Can Do This!

There is no doubt that life is a tough, competitive, and demanding endeavor. So, what do you do for the rest of your professional career? Settle for less and give up your dreams? No. You do have some big shoes to fill. Really big! Clearly you face new global challenges that previous generations did not have at your age. But let me tell you something. You were bred to run!

You are part of a nation that may have hidden under the kitchen table while virtually the entire industrialized world was at war in the 1930's, but when those bombs hit Pearl Harbor on a lazy Sunday morning on

December 7, 1941, all hell broke loose. Let there be no doubt, your parents and grandparents crawled out of their hiding places, suited up, strapped it on, kicked some serious butt, and saved the free world! Americans always have and always will figure out a way to compete, fight and win in any situation. It will be up to you to protect our nation's freedom. It is also important to remember what former President Ronald Reagan once said during the height of the Cold War:

"Freedom is never more than one generation away from extinction. We didn't pass it to our children in the bloodstream. It must be fought for, protected, and handed on for them to do the same, or one day we will spend our sunset years telling our children and our children's children what it was once like in the United States where men (and women) were free."

My generation is counting on your generation to take this state and nation to the next level for your children and grandchildren. Failure is not an option. It will take serious preparation, a smart plan and hard work. Excuses and delays are for losers, and you are not a loser. You are an American! So don't waste time. Let's get this thing cranked up!

Prepare For Challenges and Opportunities

You have many challenges ahead, and it has been said that success comes when preparation and opportunity meet. You must continue to improve your skills, knowledge, and scope of experience in an ever increasing complex and extremely competitive global economy.

I have recommended that many young professionals completing their degrees take a serious look at the opportunities available by enlisting or becoming an officer in the U.S. military. Benefits in today's military include competitive pay, healthcare, thirty days paid vacation per year, retirement, educational benefits, and many career field choices that offer excellent training as well as meaningful work experience.

Better Education and Training: Outsource-proof Yourself!

It is hard to find the time, energy and money to finish college, get that MBA or technical certification. For many it seems out of reach when balancing jobs, bills and family. Like many of you I completed my advanced degrees as a working single parent, earning a Ph.D. when I was 43. Most of the graduate students I teach are working adults, so I understand your challenges. One of the things I enjoy most about teaching college is seeing the look of achievement and satisfaction on the face of young professionals when they master a research paper and formally present their findings with energy and confidence.

The global economy is here to stay. We must improve our education system in Florida, ensuring graduates at all levels have the skills, knowledge and degree programs and areas of study that will provide them competitive advantage in securing high paying and enduring careers right here in the Sunshine State.

Seizing the Future and Reaping the Benefits

The future for young professionals must offer substantial opportunities with long term, rewarding career paths. To secure, protect and maximize your future you have to be better than the global competition. Each and every day you must focus on the tasks at hand, and have a sound goal and strategy for personal growth and development. The key to success is striving for constant, ongoing self improvement.

Be proactive. Don't just sit there quietly hoping things will work out. Look the role, act the role, feel the role, and be the role. You can and must do it!

The successful future of our young professionals is a critical piece of this "Vision for Progress and Prosperity," so get the word of this book to everyone you know!

Chapter 12
Senior Citizens: Our National Heritage

Seniors Acknowledged

It is critically important that we acknowledge the sacrifices, contributions and accomplishments of our senior citizens. After some research, I discovered that had it not been for my parents, I would not be here! (By the way, the same is true for you too.) We owe this sector of our population for our very existence as well as for the tremendous advantages they have provided us, our state, and our nation throughout their lifetimes. They must be appreciated, respected, and rewarded. Taking care of our seniors is a mainstay of this Vision.

Issues, Concerns and Needs of Our Senior Citizens

It is important for us to recognize the financial concerns of our seniors. It disgusts and saddens me to see them cheated not only by the recession, but by financial collapses that have diminished much of their life's savings. Their losses are doubly tragic because for most, their earning years are behind them, and they are unable to make up what was lost. Many of us who are still in the workplace have lost 20 to 40 % of the value in our homes, stock portfolios and 401K's. However for those of us still working, we have time to make it back. Most seniors don't have that luxury.

What Must We Do to Protect and Honor Our Seniors?

The answer is whatever it takes. Seniors are counting on us to preserve, protect and improve the nation they built and handed off to us. We must not let them down. We must keep our country strong and protect the healthcare, finances, and quality of life they helped create and deserve to enjoy. These goals will only be possible through strong economic growth, improved education and job training for all U.S. workers, and strategically aligning the healthcare system to decrease unnecessary costs. Seniors are a key piece of this "Vision for Progress and Prosperity." Not only must we protect their interests, but we must also encourage their involvement as we work together to make Florida a better place to call home.

Chapter 13
Florida's Cultural Diversity: An Area of Strength

Minority Demographics

Now more than ever before, our state and nation is a melting pot of cultures. Some demographic studies indicate that the percentages of minorities in our nation are roughly 5% Asian, 12% African American, and 18% Hispanic; the latter is our fastest growing segment. These numbers may differ from area to area, state to state, and may well be redefined in the 2010 census.

It is our diversity that helps define us as a state, and it is collectively who we are. In many ways our differences give us strengths and advantages that will play a key role in Florida's future success. It is also our array of cultures, backgrounds and languages that create challenges. How we face challenges and turn them into advantages will be important for our collective future success.

Asians

Though the Asian demographic in our state and nation is small compared to other minority groups, on a global basis Asians are considered the largest group. China and India alone comprise roughly 2.5 billion people and represent around 40% of the world's population. Add in Japan with another 250 million, and the number increases to 2.75 billion people.

Asians are having a major impact in the global economy. China is now considered by some to be the largest exporter of goods on the planet, and the U.S. is the largest purchaser of these goods. Here in Florida we have seen a significant increase in the number of physicians and engineers from India and other Asian nations. I have worked with many Florida physicians and health care professionals who are of Asian descent, and have taught many of these individuals in my MBA classes.

It should be noted here, as well as in the chapter on education, that some data denotes that Chinese students have the most school days as well as the most hours per day spent outside class on academics and study. Korea was second and Japan third, while the U.S. wasn't even in the top ten in some key categories. There is a great cultural value for academics in Asian nations that should be recognized and adopted as we make much needed upgrades to our educational system.

African Americans

This sector of our state and nation is also an important component of our society, and workforce. I was fortunate to gain a better understanding of the African American culture when I was ordered to Active Duty, to teach Army ROTC at Florida A&M University in Tallahassee. This assignment was a great learning experience for me, as it was the first time I had been a "minority" in a work environment. The President of Florida A&M University was Dr. Fred Humphries, from whom I learned a great deal. Dr. Humphries was an entrepreneur and strong activist in the nationwide recruiting of African American scholars to Florida A&M.

It was exciting to work with him in this process. We had an arrangement that if we recruited these scholars into high tech curriculums such as engineering or nursing on an Army tuition scholarship, Dr. Humphries would provide them a free Presidential room and board scholarship. As a result we became the second largest Army ROTC scholarship program in the nation, second only to Notre Dame!

During this tenure I was appointed to serve on the Faculty Senate, a University Academic Task Force, the Commencement Committee and was a Department Chair. It was great to watch the competitive spirit of these bright young students, many of who went on to be Army officers and successful business professionals.

Hispanics

The Hispanic population is a unique key piece of our population, business and culture. My discussions with Hispanic friends have provided one perspective for the difference of terms between Hispanic and Latino, at least in this geography. For some, Latinos would refer to all those of Latin decent; whereas here locally when we refer to Hispanics, we generally do not include Europeans.

In the area of the state where I live just outside Tampa, much of the construction, trade, and agricultural work forces are Hispanic. I have had the opportunity to interact with many of these individuals. They face huge obstacles in this country including citizenship and language barriers.

Cuban Sector

The population of the Cuban sector is of particular significance in Florida when compared to other areas of the nation due to the sheer numbers of Cuban Americans who make their home here. It has been a great experience to meet, work with, teach, socialize and better know this culture. Many of my colleagues, associates and students in the healthcare field are Cuban. They are some of the hardest working, performance driven and self-aware individuals I have met. And yes, in my single life I have dated some Cuban women; they are smart, meticulous, beautiful, and can speak really fast Spanish when they are upset with you! You have to bring your "A" game!

There are many Cubans living in Florida who were forced to leave their loved ones, businesses, homes, and careers behind. Arriving in the United States with few resources, they learned a new language, and began new lives. They are major contributors to our state's economy. For Cuban Americans and those they left behind, a free and democratic Cuba must be achieved now.

Speaking Spanish

Language is an area of difficulty for many of us, and can be a serious barrier. English is the primary language in the U.S., and is commonly spoken in many parts of the world. I believe if you are a U.S. citizen, or you make your permanent home here you should be able to speak English.

However, Spanish too is spoken by many around the world and is often the preferred language of the Hispanic community. So what do we do? Perhaps we should learn from other countries whose students not only speak a national language, but learn to fluently communicate in other languages as well.

As mentioned in other chapters, I have taught college and worked in the healthcare field throughout the southeast and central parts of Florida for many years. I've admired and respected Hispanic adult students I taught in MBA classes, as well as professionals I've worked with in healthcare for their mastery of both English and Spanish. As a result, I am practicing what I preach and am learning Spanish. It is not easy believe me; with genders, formal, informal, and slang I feel like I am learning four languages at once, but I am determined to succeed. However if we should meet, and you speak to me in Spanish go easy on me! All of our citizens must be equal partners in achieving this "Vision for Progress and Prosperity."

Chapter 14
Security for Our Families: Financial, Physical, Emotional

Having the peace of mind that comes from knowing that our families are financially, physically and emotionally secure is not easy to obtain or hold onto. Yet it is our collective goal. My Vision for Florida recognizes these issues and their importance.

Financial Security

This piece of the equation has been discussed and represented in other chapters, particularly those focusing on jobs, economy, training and education. Without being repetitive, it is crucial that the citizens of Florida achieve financial security. We must protect our families, homes, incomes, jobs, careers, and savings.

Physical Security

This critical issue has many parts, and has different meanings for different people. If you have ever been robbed, you know the feeling of personal invasion, helplessness and anger. Some would be frightened for their families' safety. Others would fear having personal property stolen or damaged. For others it is a combination of the two. We depend on ourselves, neighbors, and law enforcement to help provide protection. For these reasons, the right to own a firearm for protection as guaranteed by the founding fathers should not be denied to responsible citizens in our state.

Many wonder if we are safe from an attack that threatens our way of life. For these issues we rely on having a strong, ready and well-equipped National Guard, Reserve and Active Duty military force. Citizenry and local law enforcement are not properly equipped to deal with the magnitude of these threats. There are those who don't believe we need a strong national defense. Those people scare me, and their philosophy should scare you too. There have been wars, attacks and invasions throughout history. It is still going on today, as recently as 9/11.

What on earth would make us suddenly believe that the bad guys no longer want to hurt us? The vast majority of Americans don't have a U.S. Government Security Clearance, and therefore are not privy to the classified information that studies, tracks and counters these threats. If everyone in America really knew what went on in enemy circles, they'd want all the protection they could get.

The news media is not provided classified information either, and if it fell into their hands it is illegal for them to disseminate it. The reason is that our enemies watch our news and read our papers trying to gain information to use against us. Although some members of our society don't believe this goes on, it does not change the fact that it does. There are very dangerous people out there who do not play well in the sand box. Our elected leaders must understand this threat and be prepared to defeat it.

Florida is a state with enormous vulnerable borders. The federal government is responsible for protecting our borders and needs to do a better job. Perhaps the federal government should compensate Florida for costs we bear associated with this lapse in security. We must ensure our physical security and protect our state interests. We need leadership that understands this at the highest level.

Emotional Security

Emotional security comes from the confidence and knowledge that things will be alright; and is further supported by assurance that our leaders are properly looking out for us. It is knowing we will always be able to pay our bills, and meet our families' needs; knowing that our parents and children are safe, comfortable and successful; and knowing our home, investments, career, savings and businesses will be protected. We need to know that we won't just survive but thrive. Though we each seek different paths, our common link is our need for security on every level. Ensuring security for our families is a key goal of this "Vision for Progress and Prosperity."

Chapter 15
Protecting Florida's Environment

Florida is a state with a unique, delicately balanced and world class environment. According to the Florida Almanac (McGovern, 2008), Florida covers 35 million areas of land, has 1,197 miles of shoreline, 10.5 million acres of wetlands, 7,800 lakes and 16 million acres of forests. Florida is home to thousands of species of flora and fauna, many of which are endangered or threatened.

These natural resources were of such interest to me that I included an Area of Specialization in Environmental Management in my doctoral curriculum. During these studies I conducted numerous field research trips from the Panhandle to the Keys, meeting with and learning from virtually every state and federal agency involved in environmental issues in Florida. I participated in a number of on-site studies of coral reefs, beaches and shoreline, the Everglades, estuaries, aquifers, and wetland wildlife. Additionally, I later served as an Environmental Officer for the Florida National Guard. In this position I conducted an environmental inspection of every Florida Army National Guard facility in the state from Pensacola to Miami.

As a Combat Engineer in the Guard and on military Active Duty, I have been involved in funding requirements and reviewing Environmental Impact Studies and Environmental Assessments. It was in this position that I learned that there can and must be a process and resolution when it comes to creating partners in business, agriculture, and the military to protect our environment. We need better answers that solve issues, create opportunity, and protect jobs and the environment, without creating additional problems. This must and can be done. The same old rhetoric isn't helping. We need everyone working together, not against each other.

We must all be good caretakers of our priceless ecosystem. I actively support and encourage industry, agriculture and the citizens of Florida to work together to protect our natural habitat not only for today but for our future generations.

Florida Forever

"Florida Forever" is a coalition of over 125 non-profit and private organizations created in 2001 to succeed the Preservation 2000 conservation program. The annual $300 million in bonded funding had been allocated to numerous specific conservation programs in the past to help ensure the protection of the most important and threatened areas. However, in 2009 the state legislature chose not to fully fund the program, facing a multibillion dollar budget gap; an idea that may have sounded good on paper but could have dire consequences. Protecting our natural resources is a fight we can't afford to lose.

Florida's waters, timberlands, coastal ecosystems, farming and agriculture and other key resources and industries benefit from Florida Forever; I strongly support this program.

Aligning All Stakeholders

Having doctoral level research studies, professional environmental experience, being commercially involved in agriculture and being a small business owner has provided me the insight, knowledge and confidence that we can and must strategically align Florida's business and industry, agriculture, eco-tourism and natural resources into a better integrated and interoperable machine that creates jobs, promotes economic growth and protects our world class environment. These different organizations and issues are interdependent on each other and must work together with synergy for their individual and collective interests and benefits for a win-win outcome. Improving and protecting our environment is a key piece of this "Vision for Progress and Prosperity."

Chapter 16
Importance of the Media

In any organization "communications" are essential. I learned this lesson well when serving as a Communications Officer at three levels in the military. In fact, in military operations the methodology of "shoot, move and communicate" is paramount. In today's high speed technological world we have come to expect and demand immediate communication in every aspect of life, business and information management. Our dependence on all forms of communication is at a new high.

Our expectation and need for instantaneous, up to the minute, and complete information has placed tremendous demands on all outlets of the media. They must be acknowledged and applauded for the service they bring us. They risk their safety to investigate and report on storms, crimes, and wars. We expect them to be experts in every field of study, and provide immediate reporting on any and all events. This can be an impossible task, yet they are there, working to deliver the news.

We will need the media in all future efforts, giving us cutting edge advantages in response to events, opportunities and danger. We need them to sort out hard facts from rumors and fiction. We need them to control news that could endanger our security, such as the release of "leaked" classified information that would be of great value to our enemies. To do so requires restraint, discipline, and integrity.

Additionally we need them to give fair balance, equal reporting and air time to all political candidates running for key offices. The media has a huge impact on our perception and opinion of politics and candidates running for office. We need them to help level the playing field of public knowledge and exposure to the candidates, and not simply sell air time to those with the most resources for political advertisements. Otherwise voters are left to the mercy of big money politics as well as the clout of political parties. This will be a difficult task, as the media needs to make a profit like any other business.

Since the media is our primary source of information, they must be honest brokers and educators by providing us with the entire and factual picture. By providing fair balance to all candidates, voters will not be left to swim through the murky waters of big money politics. Doing so may be in their interests as well, as the public quickly wearies of the plethora of negative political ads during election season. Many citizens don't even want to turn on their televisions after political ads go into attack mode. Who can blame them?

Because the news media is our lifeblood to information, we the voters need political news that is unvarnished and truthful, so we can make informed decisions about the future of our families, businesses and state. We need news that is above the mudslinging and accusations of the political process. We also should insist that the political candidates behave like the leaders they wish to be, and stick to solutions for the issues that affect us all. They should not create a media circus with mudslinging and character assassinations. Should we surmise candidates will act the same way behind closed doors, once in office, as they do while campaigning to get in office?

Providing a fair balance and accuracy of information that separates fact from rumor is essential in this "Vision for Progress and Prosperity."

Chapter 17
Real World Experience and Leadership to Strategically Align Florida for Long Term Success and Sustainability

Role of Leaders

Many years of civilian education, military training, and professional experience has taught me significant lessons about life. When I was in Officer Candidate School (OCS) training to be a military officer they told us we were learning some of life's most valuable lessons, and how to apply them so everyone benefits. Two of the most critical leadership concepts they emphasized over and over were "mission accomplishment" and "take care of the troops!"

Genuine concern for people, their interests and well being, while achieving the task at hand is what leadership is all about. Leaders must be fair, knowledgeable and people of action. They cannot be afraid to fight alongside their troops in the midst of battles that must be fought. True leaders must be willing to lead the charge to victory from the front.

After earning a Ph.D. in Management, I completed the Harvard University "Senior Executive Leadership Program" at the JFK School of Government. The curriculum utilized a number of case studies that were "declassified" documents from the War College. Being a War College graduate prior to completing the Harvard program, I gained an even higher respect for my senior level military training and schooling, realizing the education I received there was absolutely world class.

The Department of Defense is one of the largest organizations in the U.S. involving a million people, billion dollar decisions, three quarters of a trillion dollar budget, planning and conducting missions with extremely serious consequences and comprehensive global responsibilities. That is why senior military officers are often asked to serve on corporate boards immediately after retirement from military service. While serving as a Colonel, I was fortunate to have been given assignments involved at the highest levels. This included Pentagon meetings, strategic decision making, and implementation. I learned critical lessons from some of the very best in that five-sided building.

What Does "Strategically Aligned" Mean and Why Do It?

That is a great question. We all hear this term thrown around in business and government. It has been used several times in this book. Ok, what does it really mean? In simple terms, strategic alignment is the process of ensuring that the entire organization is on the same sheet of music, doing the right things and heading straight to the future target; that all goals, strategies, tactics, actions, programs, resources and efforts are coordinated and managed for maximum results and minimal waste throughout the organization.

When working on my doctoral dissertation, I had to conduct many field researches into business and government management as well as operations. I attempted to choose "best of class" industry competitors, contacted them, and set up appointments to visit their facilities. While there I observed their operations, talked with their employees and managers, and had private one-on-ones with senior executives including CEOs. It was interesting to note how cooperative most were in granting access (especially after I told them I was writing a dissertation, and wanted to learn from the best). I always asked senior executives what the key was to their career success, as well as the key to their organization's future success. This was before the term "strategically aligned" became popular.

The most common response I heard was how absolutely essential it is to have everyone in the organization share the same vision, understand their individual roles in that vision, and to ensure that all activities, resources, and efforts are focused on achieving those goals and objectives required for the organization to reach the vision. Yep, that pretty much defines strategic alignment. Not a textbook definition, but a real world definition.

Florida Strategically Aligned

Future Plan for Florida Concept. This is what my Vision for the "Right Future for Florida" encompasses. We must bring all workers, government, resources and effort to bear in an organized plan that gets Florida and its citizens to where we want to be. Ok, now let's start putting this plan together.

How Do We Get Strategically Aligned? Now that we know what it means and why we do it, the question is *how* do we do it? First, we have to know how to identify the **right** vision (or desired future state). We can't get where we want to be if we don't know where it is; and we can't become what we want to be if we don't know what it is.

True strategic alignment is a very complex and intensive process, which is why all the steps are specifically outlined in Chapter 17. Once we identify our vision we must get everyone involved, and to do this we must get the word to everyone. Tell your family, friends, colleagues and associates to read this book. It is intentionally inexpensive and only takes about an hour or two to read. For many it may help change their lives.

Involving All Stakeholders: What Can You Do? It is important to involve everyone with an interest in the fight. In business we generally identify stakeholders as stockholders (owners), employees, customers, suppliers and creditors of an organization. In this case the stakeholders are you and me, the citizens of Florida. We must take ownership and control of our lives and families' future. We cannot allow political parties to select our candidates without meaningful primary elections. We must have serious say in which leaders will ultimately lead Florida into the future. Maybe as citizens we've avoided being involved in the process. Perhaps we've been too busy to research the job requirements for an elected office and compare those to the credentials of the candidates.

We can't continue this practice. We must be a wise hiring authority. An official elected for one job does not always qualify them to perform another job. Think about it like this; are bankers and lawyers interchangeable? How about pilots and bartenders? Get the picture? That being said, prior election to public office does not always mean that the

119

individual is qualified to occupy a higher office than previously held. It often just means that voters are familiar with the candidate's name.

Dirty Politics

In the case of bad press, it is important to know the source of the report. Was it levied by a political opponent? Is the report factual or just an accusation to throw us off the right path? Was it from someone wanting attention or harboring ill will? It's a shame that there are high quality citizens who will not consider running for political office primarily because of the threat of accusations, name calling, and ruined reputations that have become a part of the political landscape.

I've had many successful business and military leaders tell me if you haven't done anything wrong, never been accused of a bad decision, never made a mistake, or never made anyone mad, you haven't done much. I'll say it again. We're all sick and tired of character assassinations during political campaigns. Give us the individual who faces difficult issues, rather than avoiding controversy. This is why I clearly stated where I stand on issues and my Vision for Florida in Chapter 1 of this book.

We as a people must recognize there will always be charges, jealousy, envy, dislike and animosity for people who take a stand, fight for a cause, are in a position of responsibility, and try to make a positive difference in the world, especially if they "go against the status quo." People of action are often misunderstood, their intentions misinterpreted or falsely viewed. This is the risk that leaders face, and the main reason many politicians avoid decisions that need to be made, especially if the subject matter is controversial. It takes brave individuals of exceptional character to stand up for what is right in a volatile political climate.

In Officer Candidate School (OCS) they taught us to make decisions, and take action because doing nothing gets people hurt. I am somewhat encouraged by evidence that some political party circles and county party leaders are becoming more supportive of this voter uprising. Be part of this voice. An example of this would be the energy of the campaign of Marco Rubio, who has demonstrated that a conservative can gain the support of the voters even against a political party leader and incumbent.

The recruiting and electing of government officials who truly possess the real world experience, expertise and proven leadership to run our state is a top priority of this "Vision for Progress and Prosperity."

Chapter 18
The Right Plan for Lasting Progress and Prosperity
to Ensure We get Where We Want to Be!

Developing a Plan for Progress and Prosperity
that "Fits and Lasts"

A common buzzword in politics is "change." Perhaps instead change
should be expanded to mean "effective change with strategic fit for
success." Again, it is expected for this book to come under scrutiny and
attack by some politicians and/or their representatives, as it examines and
questions the status quo. Let's tell them to "bring it on," in a face-to-face
public forum. No hiding solo behind TV cameras, radio, or newspaper
headlines and no political party or campaign representative fighting their
battles for them. We need less dirty politics, and more answers for our
state-wide issues and problems.

I will predict that as this book reaches Florida voters in an election
year, the demographic groups specifically addressed here (displaced
workers, single parents, military veterans, young professional, minorities,
senior citizens, and business owners) will suddenly become a focal point
for the candidates. Of course they will assure us that our needs have
always been their primary concern, and they will suddenly present us with
answers to these problems.

Why all this interest and sudden ability to solve Florida's issues now; especially from those currently holding office? Note the word "primary." Therein may be the real focus, as in "primary elections."

Where have they been the last several years? If they have been on top of the issues, then why are we still struggling with the same old difficulties? They can't have it both ways. If they've been in the driver's seat and our problems still exist, they weren't particularly interested to begin with; or they haven't a clue how to fix what is broken. Now a number of them want the voters to promote them to higher elected offices. Does this make sense? Would they care about us if they didn't need our votes?

We require results, not talk. We need engaged leadership.

I have been writing this book for the last eight to ten months, and it reflects my experiences gained in various fields of academic, professional and military service. During the book's developmental stage, I sent drafts of the manuscript to numerous subject matter experts and other professionals for their review and analysis. It will be interesting to see if any political campaigns adjust their positions or strategy to closely to either reflect this book and its contents, or oppose them.

Changing Global Middle Class

This is one of the longest chapters in the book. It identifies the right methodology, processes, and components critical to successfully develop and implement a winning strategic plan for Florida's success and prosperity in today's rapid paced and dynamic global economy. Let there

123

be no doubt, today's world is much more complex, and competitive than ever before. The largest nations on earth are now some of the fastest developing and emerging economies.

To provide some comparison of what we are up against, keep in mind the United States comprises approximately 5% of the world's population, while, as previously stated, China and India combined make up roughly 40%; or eight times more people. Some studies rank China as the largest exporter of goods on the planet, yet it has extremely low wages and virtually ineffective patent laws. This combined with data demonstrating that Chinese and Korean students now have the most school days, as well as the most time spent outside the classroom on academic study gives us valuable insight. We can see how things are changing, where they are heading, and how much some nations have recently advanced in the areas of manufacturing, exportation and education.

One study cited by the USDA states that China now has over 290 million middle class citizens, which is becoming comparable to the United States, with India having over 91 million. This data indicates China and India combined have more middle class citizens than the United States. As a benchmark, Russia has only 66 million middle class citizens, Brazil 58 million, Mexico 45 million, and Korea with 44 million.

Florida's Failing Education System

As discussed in Chapters 1 and 5, a serious concern is that Florida ranked 47th out of 50 states in 2009 ACT scores, which unlike the SAT includes science testing. ACT and SAT are standardized national tests

124

administered in high school, and used by colleges and universities for admission determinations. FCAT scores have little, if any use when it comes to college admission, even at Florida colleges and universities. FCAT scores are used to evaluate Florida schools, thus schools have focused on teaching to FCAT standards instead of the skills and curriculum needed for students to gain college admission and perform on a college level. As previously mentioned, these performance measures must include student scores on national standardized tests such as ACT and SAT.

The average ACT scores for 2009 graduating seniors from Florida high schools was 19.4, while the average ACT score for the freshman class at the University of Florida in 2009 was about 26 to 29. This is one reason why so many Florida students can't get into their own state colleges and universities. They don't score well enough on the tests that matter most. Our state has many bright, exceptional students. However, **a state average ranking of 47th out of 50 states clearly screams the message that we are not getting the job done for the majority. What a horrible waste of talent, and potential. Together we must finally fix this!**

For many years I have pleaded for a strategically aligned education system from kindergarten through college and graduate school, to provide better curriculums and seamless transitions at every juncture. This move will better prepare our students for college or tech schools, the workplace and life in general.

In my experience teaching at many colleges and universities throughout Florida, my colleagues and I continue to have serious concerns about how much difficulty some college students have writing a paragraph, solving math problems, or finding good peer reviewed, academic quality research material.

Together We Can and Must Fix This!

The take home message of this book is that we must be aware of our competition with other states and the world, as well as what we must do to secure lasting prosperity, positioning Florida in its rightful leadership role. Join with me, and together we can and will get this fixed. I am out here living and fighting these issues with you. I am not watching you fight them. Therein is the difference between us and many politicians. Let's join together and take back control of our lives, our state and our future and go win this thing!

Methodology for Strategic Planning

Mission: What is Our Purpose? Mission statements should clearly identify the primary purpose of an organization or entity. In other words why does it exist, and what is its purpose? Mission statements, like vision statements are frequently vague and non-specific. They may be constructed of words that project images or values that are admirable and socially correct. After all, how can anyone not like mom, apple pie and the American way? However, they publicly avoid specifics and performance objectives that would create accountability of the desired end state outcomes. Those real world performance measures are kept behind closed doors, or saved for the board room.

In the case of government the mission may have legal definitions by statutes, however those entrusted with jobs in public service, and especially **those in elected leadership positions work for the citizens**. Elected officials must not simply give lip service regarding Florida's needs. They need to get busy and help us. We should expect our elected leaders to put aside political partisanship and self-interest to better serve the citizens who elect and pay them.

Governments must provide an environment that is supportive of our democratic society, public well-being, safety and business interests. This must include a business friendly atmosphere that will not only allow, but facilitate Florida businesses to survive, grow and prosper against all competition, both foreign and domestic. The future success of our families, communities and state depend on it!

Current State: Where Are We Now? It is a smart business methodology to clearly, factually and accurately identify an organization's current state or situation. This can be observed by the delivery of the State of the Union Address each year by the President of the United States, providing Congress and the American people a report on the condition of our country. One of the most accepted practices utilized to determine an organization or entities' current state is to conduct a situational analysis consisting of three key components:

A.) *SWOT Analysis* identifies the strengths and weaknesses in the internal environment, and the opportunities and threats in the external environment. The military refers to this as "situational awareness," as it constantly identifies and evaluates one's own situation as well as that of the opposition and the world around us.
Some of the biggest mistakes in history have been the result of not knowing the competition, and underestimating what the organization was up against.

B.) *Market Analysis* evaluates the marketplace, industry target segment, competition, and customer base, in which an organization competes and must survive, thus providing insight on how to best meet end user requirements and secure their business.

C.) *Financial Analysis* of one's own organization provides information as to the current financial condition to include debts, assets, credit status, etc., and includes measurement indicators such as balance sheet, cash flow, income statement, profit and loss and key financial ratios. This information is critical in order for an organization to make sound business decisions.

Vision: Where Do We Want to Be? It is very important for any organization or individual to have a well defined vision of where it wants to go. Again, it is hard to get where you want to go if you don't know where that is! To properly establish a vision, or desired future state, requires in-depth knowledge and understanding of one's current situation, as well as competition in the marketplace, customer/end user needs, and the environment in which we live and operate. That is why we discussed this in the preceding section on situational analysis. A vision should be challenging, yet achievable. It should define specific desired outcomes as well as end-state goals.

A vision must be forward looking and include effective analysis of the future landscape, marketplace, competition and customer needs. Otherwise it will be out of date or off the mark, either before or when it is achieved. Many of us have heard this referred to as "a day late and a dollar short." We must prepare for the fast changes in products, services, and technologies. Our job training, educational system, and businesses must meet future challenges from domestic and global competition, and at the same time exploit and secure the future opportunities by providing superior products, services and proprietary competitive advantages.

Again, this task will demand that we do better in preparing our students and workers by encouraging them to be determined, innovative and confident.

Gap Analysis: The Difference Between Where We Are and Where We Want to Be. Before strategic/organizational goals and objectives can be effectively identified, a gap analysis must be conducted to clearly identify the difference in current or present state (where we are now, as identified by the situational analysis), and the vision/desired state (where we want to be).

Gap analysis is like buying an airline ticket. You have to know your departing city (current state), and the city to where you are flying (vision or desired future state). Strategic or organizational goals must be the things identified by the gap analysis (measuring the difference between where we are and where we want to be) that must be achieved to reach the vision. Simply setting achievable strategic goals will not ensure reaching the vision if they do not eliminate the gap. This mistake can leave organizations wondering what went wrong when they achieve their goals and not their vision.

A real world example may be the rising FCAT scores, in contrast to the falling ACT scores. It is ACT scores that are used by colleges and universities for choosing which students to accept, not FCAT scores, which are used to measure school performance. We must have the right strategic goals that will take us to the right vision. College entrance exam scores are far more valuable to a student's future than FCAT scores.

Research and Analysis: Utilize Quality Research to Choose Best Options. Any sound methodology will consist of quality Research & Analysis (R&A). We will now identify some of the components of this process.

Purpose of Research and Analysis. When conducting organizational analysis and making business decisions, quality information and accurate interpretations are critical. It is not smart to make business decisions with poor or biased information. Therefore, every effort should be made to ensure the quality and usefulness of the information we utilize. So, how do we do that? Let's move on to discuss this key question; after all it's our tax dollars and future at stake here.

What is Peer Review, and What Data or Reports Can I Believe?
Most of us have heard the old saying "garbage in – garbage out." This means that if the information used for decisions is not high quality, then our resulting decisions will be of poor quality. So, the big question is "how do I know the difference?"

One of the things I learned while earning a Ph.D., chairing university MBA thesis committees, discussing clinical studies with physicians, and serving as lead investigator for a Department of Defense global study on an issue of U.S. National Security, is that you must have a "sound methodology" for data and information collection. That methodology must utilize critical processes in order to ensure only the best information is being used, and that it is free of bias (prejudice, favoritism, personal agenda or opinion). Just because something is in print or broadcast on television does not always ensure accuracy.

When researching information it is important to review the credentials of the author, determine that the information is peer reviewed, as well as knowing the agenda and motivation of the author. In the writing of this book, I had many discussions with subject matter experts (SME) on the topics addressed, and even asked many to review these findings and recommendations so as to get expert review in each subject or issue. Though even experts don't agree on all issues and options, consensus of opinion of experts should be used.

Remember that by their nature, some elected officials, (particularly state and U.S. representatives) may be biased in their views, as their jobs are to represent a certain sector of the population. As a result, their outlook may be narrowed and not best for the state as a whole. The honest brokers must be those holding state-wide office such as Governor or U.S. Senator. In the case of Senators, they can be influenced to vote along national political party lines. This leaves the Governor as our best statewide voice.

Quality Research Data Collection and Analysis. Data collection is a major component of these processes, yet as we know data and numbers can be misinterpreted or even manipulated, leading to wrong conclusions. In order to prevent misinformation, either intentionally (bias) or unintentionally (error), data collection must possess a methodology involving critical processes and quality control to include accuracy, practicality, validity, reliability, bias control and statistical significance. In layman's words we might think of these terms as follows:

1.) Accuracy, meaning the data collected is correct and factual.

2.) Practicality, meaning the data and research has value and relevance to the study.

3.) Validity, meaning we accurately measured what we intended (avoid error).

4.) Reliability, meaning if other researchers repeated our work, they would come to the same consensus or conclusions.

5.) Bias control eliminates contamination of the data by our own (or the researchers) beliefs, agenda, needs or desired conclusions.

6.) Statistical significance allows us to assign a numerical value (sometimes referred to as "P Factor") which identifies or measures the odds that our conclusions and findings were the result of random chance. P Values equal to or less than 0.5 (P = or < 0.5) are considered to be statistically significant, which could be interpreted to mean that the chance of the findings or conclusions being due to random chance is 1 out of 20 or less, thus our conclusions are considered accurate and not just coincidence. Ok, still awake? Let's move on then.

Set Strategic Goals: What Do We Need to Do to Get Where We Want to Be? As previously mentioned, strategic or organizational goals must be derived from the gap analysis, and must be what needs to be achieved in order to reach the vision. In other words, doing the right things to get where we want to be.

The Strategic Goals in My Vision For Florida Must Include:

Creating a prospering and durable economy (sustainability) and a positive business environment with **low taxes and tax incentives that will support, create, and bring jobs and economic growth in small business and industry to Florida**. Furthermore it must protect and capitalize on Florida's proprietary advantages in weather, eco-tourism, agriculture, geographical location and size, population and work force. Specifics include and are not limited to:

1.) **Robust job growth and sustainability** in business and industry to include healthcare, education, energy, manufacturing and technology; as well as enhanced job training for displaced workers

133

by providing the skills and knowledge for today's careers and future job security.

2.) **A significantly improved education system** that is strategically aligned and seamless from kindergarten through college and graduate school, providing curriculums and degrees that will be in demand for future jobs. It is crucial for industry to have increased input into curriculum development, and **increased job placement** through expanded college internship courses.

3.) **Ensure military bases and VA facilities and hospitals remain open** and operating; thus creating jobs and **providing the needed services our military veterans and their families were promised.** Protect veteran pensions and retirements.

4.) **Create and sustain opportunities that provide a positive future for our young professionals and their families**. These are our future workers, leaders and heads of household. They must have the opportunities to succeed, be able to capitalize upon these opportunities and overcome the challenges ahead.

5.) **A high quality of life for our senior citizens** who worked and built this great state and nation. These objectives must include quality health care, and protection of their homes, retirements and pensions.

6.) **A healthcare system that provides affordable, available and high quality healthcare to all Floridians** by integrating healthcare providers (doctors, hospitals, pharmacies, labs), healthcare payers (insurance companies, Medicare, Medicaid, other government), healthcare vendors (manufacturers of equipment and pharmaceuticals, etc.) into a more interoperable system that improves the quality and cost effectiveness of health care.

7.) **Legal system reform that weeds out frivolous law suits and provides a business friendly atmosphere** to grow Florida's economy and job base, as well as helping **keep doctors and hospitals serving Florida patients**.

8.) **Accessible and affordable insurance for our homes, cars, businesses and healthcare** with transparency of rates and coverages.

9.) **Security of our homes, neighborhoods, and borders** must continue to improve. **Foreclosures must be resolved and better prevented in the future.**

10.) **Immigration concerns must be addressed, to reach a resolution that is just**, distributing the financial burden of taxation equitably to everyone who enjoys the fantastic advantages of living and working in the great state of Florida.

11.) **Develop and implement an effective master plan and strategy for Florida** that integrates and brings to bear all instruments, capabilities, advantages and human resources in a strategically aligned and tactically sound effort. Also more infrastructure development to maximize value, as well as **achieve the desired**

end-state outcomes of progress and lasting prosperity for
Florida. No one can be left out. Everyone must be enabled to have
a role, contributing what he or she does best in a comprehensive
community effort.

12.) **Ensure all programs and projects involving tax dollars are
truly strategically aligned with the goals and Vision for
Florida.** This is an area where government must be more efficient,
less wasteful and **operate on a balanced state budget**. Spending
money that will not provide desired end-state outcomes or desired
future state goals is a luxury we can't afford.

13.) **Leadership in Florida state government that not only
incorporates and coordinates priorities and efforts of
government at all levels (city, county, state), but also
strategically aligns these efforts to ensure interoperability that
best meet the needs of Floridians.**

14.) **Buy-in, active support, and unity from all of Florida's twenty
five U.S. Congressional representatives as well as both U.S.
Senators** is sorely needed. Our Congressional leaders must present
a united front, and have a strong say in Washington about what is
best for Florida. They need to act collectively in Florida's best
interests, remembering **they work for the people of Florida, and
not for a political party.**

Needs Assessment: What Resources and Capabilities Do We Need?
A "needs assessment" must be included in any strategic plan, as it identifies the resources and capabilities required to achieve our strategic goals and desired end-state outcomes. We will break the needs assessment resource requirements into material and non-material solutions.

Material and Non-material Solutions. Resources are limited in any organization. Therefore, identifying the resources (needs) that an organization will require to achieve its goals and vision is critical. To achieve maximum results, this process must effectively include both material and non-material solutions. Material solutions require new or additional resources, while non-material solutions require better utilization and less waste of resources that have already been budgeted for and allocated.

Non-material solutions should be always be utilized first, as these are resources that have already been provided. It is amazing what organizations are able to do with their current resources if they have no other option. In my Vision for Florida, non-material solutions are a necessity in achieving the goals identified in this book; with proper management they often work better than simply throwing money at a problem. I believe that every effort must be exhausted to ensure all existing state resources are utilized before any material solutions (more tax dollars) are requested. This is a management practice I learned well while serving on a strategic Executive Steering Committee at the Pentagon involving billions of dollars.

Obviously, at times additional resources are required. Money is a resource requirement, of which state taxes are the primary source. The best way to ensure a good tax base is to ensure financial health and success of the tax income sources. Breaking the backs of taxpayers and businesses is a prescription for failure. Taxes must be low. Small business, industry, and the citizens of Florida must be protected from tax increases and tax-inflation. Artificially increased property taxes are a recent example of tax-inflation, as well as the unfair burden they place on property owners.

There are those who will argue that without increased tax revenues, services will suffer (as discussed in previous chapters). We will exercise prudence to ensure quality education, security (police, fire, emergency), and other vital services are protected. Increases like the recent escalation in government property tax income that greatly exceeded the growth of personal income shouldn't have happened in the first place, and must never happen again. There was a sound reason for the "Save Our Homes" amendment which should not be circumvented by tax increase loopholes, such as playing games with terms such as "recapture" or the millage rates county governments assess on the taxable value of our homes. When property values go down, so should property taxes.

Some of our elected officials would tax us into the ground if allowed. They must remember to whom they are accountable. We need governance that maximizes stakeholder (you and me) value and interests just like in the business world. Government on any level should **not** require double-digit budget increases to maintain a constant quality of service, especially during times of low to moderate inflation. This is an example of when non-material solutions must be better utilized. We all need to live within our means, government included.

Ok, let's take a look at developing a strategic plan next.

The Strategic Plan: Strategies and Tactics to Achieve Our Strategic Goals. Once an organization has properly identified the strategic goals required to achieve its vision, and has secured the needs assessment requirements (resources, money, technology, human resources, etc) to achieve these goals, the next step is to develop a strategic plan that pulls it all together. Simply put, this plan should state the vision and strategic goals for the entire organization, the strategies to achieve these goals and the tactical plan to put the strategies into action as follows:

1.) Identify the different role of all functional departments in each strategic goal.

2.) Create and state the functional area / supporting strategies that each area of the organization will use to achieve their piece of each strategic goal.

3.) Strategically align these efforts in unison for maximum synergy and resource utilization.

4.) Establish a tactical plan comprised of actions and programs that will put all the strategies into action in action in a highly organized effort.

Implementation Plan: Putting the Plan into Action. Now it is time to execute. The best-laid plans are ineffective without good execution and implementation. Anything less will ensure failure. It is often due to poor execution where organizations lose opportunities, waste resources and personnel, and fall short of their goals. The effort and coordination to put the strategic plan into action is done with a comprehensive, detailed and published Implementation Plan which is distributed throughout the organization. This Implementation Plan will:

1.) Identify the desired end-state outcomes.

2.) Require placement of the right people in the right jobs ensuring everyone is properly positioned, then assigning responsibilities.

3.) Launch tactical plans to put all strategies into motion by initiating actions and programs of all functional areas and personnel.

4.) Establish and monitor performance measures and time frames.

5.) Manage resources to minimize waste and defects through proven processes such as Total Quality Management (TQM) and Six Sigma (defect elimination).

6.) Routinely monitor progress and make corrections as needed with programs such as PERT (Performance Evaluation and Review Technique).

It will be interesting to see if any political candidates will attempt to discredit this information. After all, if they agree with what's been written, they'll have to explain why problems and issues haven't been solved under their watch. Again, let's distinguish personal attacks from the issues and problems we face. We need solutions and not finger pointing.

Let's see. What is the unemployment rate in Florida right now? What are the property taxes on that home you want? What was the average ACT score of graduating high seniors in Florida this year and why did it continue dropping to the point that we now rank 47th out of 50 states? Why is Florida's population no longer growing?
Let the games begin!

The use of a comprehensive and sound methodology will form the basis for this "Vision for Prosperity and Progress."

Chapter 19

Implementation and Moving Forward: What to Change, What to Change to, and How to Implement the Change

What to Change?

First and foremost any changes made must be the right changes. How do we know what those changes should be? When I attended the Harvard Senior Executive Leadership curriculum, this was one of four core areas of emphasis. It is an area of study I teach in Operations Management and Systems Thinking courses. Quite simply, the root cause of the problem must be accurately determined first. Organizations sometimes mistakenly identify only the surface symptoms, and then unwisely proceed to make changes, assuming they've discovered the real problem as well as a viable solution. Making changes that only affect surface symptoms but don't attack the root cause of a problem will never yield success.

What to Change To?

This is also a critical decision. If we don't change to a better way of doing things that goes to the heart of a problem and corrects the shortfall, then we won't be able to fix the problem. Therefore, we must change to a better course of action alternative that fixes the root cause of the problem and doesn't create new problems in the wake of the old ones. In other words, fix what's broke and don't break something else that isn't already broken!

To recap, we need to change to:

1.) Better jobs that are in demand now, will last into the future, and are outsource proof.

2) An economy that is more robust, durable, and better capable of handling recessions.

3.) An education system that is strategically aligned from kindergarten through college and graduate school which provides the knowledge, skills, and degrees that the future jobs will require and is more in demand with business and industry.

4.) A business friendly legal system and environment with low taxes, and a state government that encourages small business development, entrepreneurship, and attracts large and small industry that will bring jobs and resources to Florida.

5.) Dependable and affordable health, car and property insurance.

6.) Local and state government fiscal responsibility, ultimately protecting citizens from excessive tax increases while providing key services.

How to Implement the Desired Change?

This is always a serious challenge. Organizations are resistant to change, which is often the reason why changes have not already been made; this in spite of the fact that those in the know are acutely aware that improvements are needed. In industry when organizational or strategic level change is needed, new CEOs and executives are hired. In the case of Florida, it is time to have new leadership at the top of state government.

Continuing to re-elect the same officials who are content going along with the status quo will not achieve this desperately needed change. We need new leadership that does not have the burdensome baggage of owed favors to a political party or special interest groups. It is time to clean house and bring in new blood to the Governor's Cabinet with a "Bold, New, Serious Vision for Progress and Prosperity That Will Position Florida in Our Rightful Leadership Role for Long Term Success!" Accurately identifying and fixing the root cause of problems is at the core of this "Vision for Progress and Prosperity."

Chapter 20
Conclusions and Closing Comments

My friends and fellow Floridians, you now know my "Bold, New, Serious Vision for Florida." As with most things worthwhile, this will not be easy to achieve; however it should be achieved, can be achieved, and must be achieved! Floridians don't have the luxury of waiting around until the current elected officials in Tallahassee start doing their jobs. We need new leadership that works for us, experiences our concerns and knows what its like to walk in our shoes.

I have spent the last twenty years of my life in the Sunshine State. I raised my son here, and like many parents watched him overcome adversity and mistakes to become a highly successful man. He is a product of both the failings as well as the tremendous opportunities of our education system. I want to make serious improvements in education that will build upon the advantages and correct the shortfalls that now exist, for the benefit of our future generations' academic and career endeavors.

I love this state, and it is the place that I call home. It took a lot of effort, planning and risk taking for my son and me to come here. I remember watching Florida weather reports on freezing mornings back in Missouri, knowing that we were meant to be a part of this.

Florida is a special place and has been incredibly good to my family. I want only the very best for this state and its citizens. Each day, I see so much untapped potential.

I have experienced some of the very best times of my life here. I enjoy the beauty of natural treasures such as the Gulf of Mexico, Florida sunsets, and our beautiful beaches. I'm thankful that I'm a part of all this natural wonder.

So that we will be able to continue to enjoy the lives we have come to expect in the Sunshine State, we must all invest in our future. In this book I've outlined what I believe is lacking, and what it will take to bring about the right change to position Florida for long term success and our rightful leadership role in the nation and in the world.

If what I've said makes sense to you, then it's time to get everyone you know on board with this "Bold, New, Serious Vision for Florida." Elected officials work for us, are paid by us, and must represent us. They need to be reminded of it. Let's make some serious noise! Get this word and book out there: texting, emailing, talking, MySpace, Facebook, and Twitter; let's see what you got! I'm ready if you are.

Together we can be a force to be reckoned with. Join with me and let's get this thing done for those we love, those yet to come, and for the state we all call home. Let's fulfill this "Vision for Progress and Prosperity to Position Florida in Our Rightful Leadership Role for Long-term Success!"

- Mike (Bill) McCalister

http://www.MikeMcCalister.com